LEARNING RESOURCES CENTER
CRABBE LIBRARY
EASTERN KENTUCKY UNIVERSITY
RICHMOND, KY

INTRODUCING ISSUES WITH OPPOSING VIEWPOINTS®

Endangered Species

Lauri S. Friedman, *Book Editor*

GREENHAVEN PRESS
A part of Gale, Cengage Learning

Detroit • New York • San Francisco • New Haven, Conn • Waterville, Maine • London

Elizabeth Des Chenes, *Managing Editor*

© 2012 Greenhaven Press, a part of Gale, Cengage Learning

Gale and Greenhaven Press are registered trademarks used herein under license.

For more information, contact:
Greenhaven Press
27500 Drake Rd.
Farmington Hills, MI 48331-3535
Or you can visit our Internet site at gale.cengage.com

ALL RIGHTS RESERVED.
No part of this work covered by the copyright herein may be reproduced, transmitted, stored, or used in any form or by any means graphic, electronic, or mechanical, including but not limited to photocopying, recording, scanning, digitizing, taping, Web distribution, information networks, or information storage and retrieval systems, except as permitted under Section 107 or 108 of the 1976 United States Copyright Act, without the prior written permission of the publisher.

For product information and technology assistance, contact us at

Gale Customer Support, 1-800-877-4253
For permission to use material from this text or product, submit all requests online at www.cengage.com/permissions

Further permissions questions can be e-mailed to permissionrequest@cengage.com

Articles in Greenhaven Press anthologies are often edited for length to meet page requirements. In addition, original titles of these works are changed to clearly present the main thesis and to explicitly indicate the author's opinion. Every effort is made to ensure that Greenhaven Press accurately reflects the original intent of the authors. Every effort has been made to trace the owners of copyrighted material.

Cover image © Dr. Morley Read/Shutterstock.com.

LIBRARY OF CONGRESS CATALOGING-IN-PUBLICATION DATA

Endangered species / [edited by] Lauri S. Friedman.
 p. cm. -- (Introducing issues with opposing viewpoints)
 Summary: "Endangered Species: Is Species Extinction a Serious Problem?; What Are the Most Significant Threats to Endangered Species?; How Should Humans Respond to Species Decline?"-- Provided by publisher.
 Includes bibliographical references and index.
 ISBN 978-0-7377-5676-0 (hardback)
 1. Endangered species--Juvenile literature. 2. Nature conservation--Juvenile literature. I. Friedman, Lauri S.
 QH75.E647 2011
 333.95'22--dc23
                                                                                    2011021324

Printed in the United States of America
1 2 3 4 5 6 7 15 14 13 12 11

Contents

Foreword 5
Introduction 7

Chapter 1: Is Species Extinction a Serious Problem?

1. Mass Species Extinction Is Imminent 12
   Elizabeth Kolbert

2. Predictions of Mass Extinction Are Unfounded 20
   Stephen Budiansky

3. Biodiversity Loss Has Disastrous Consequences for Humankind 28
   Richard Conniff

4. The Threat of Biodiversity Loss Is Exaggerated 36
   Doug L. Hoffman

5. The IUCN Red List Is the World's Best Measure of Extinction Risk 43
   J.C. Vie, Craig Hilton-Taylor, and Simon N. Stuart

6. The IUCN Red List Is a Flawed Measure of Extinction Risk 50
   Agence France-Presse (AFP)

Chapter 2: What Are the Most Significant Threats to Endangered Species?

1. Climate Change Is a Significant Threat to Plant and Animal Species 55
   International Council for Local Environmental Initiatives (ICLEI)

2. Plant and Animal Species Can Adapt to Climate Change 63
   Josef Reichholf, interviewed by Spiegel

3. Offshore Oil Drilling Endangers Wildlife 70
   Julia Whitty

4. The Benefits of Offshore Oil Drilling Outweigh the Risks to Wildlife 78
   Ronald Bailey

Chapter 3: How Should Humans Respond to Species Decline?

1. The Endangered Species Act Is Effective   86
   National Wildlife Federation

2. The Endangered Species Act Is Not Effective   93
   PR Newswire

3. The Giant Panda Should Be Left to Go Extinct   97
   Chris Packham

4. The Giant Panda Should Not Be Left to Go Extinct   102
   Simon Usborne

Facts About Endangered Species	108
Organizations to Contact	112
For Further Reading	120
Index	125
Picture Credits	132

Foreword

Indulging in a wide spectrum of ideas, beliefs, and perspectives is a critical cornerstone of democracy. After all, it is often debates over differences of opinion, such as whether to legalize abortion, how to treat prisoners, or when to enact the death penalty, that shape our society and drive it forward. Such diversity of thought is frequently regarded as the hallmark of a healthy and civilized culture. As the Reverend Clifford Schutjer of the First Congregational Church in Mansfield, Ohio, declared in a 2001 sermon, "Surrounding oneself with only like-minded people, restricting what we listen to or read only to what we find agreeable is irresponsible. Refusing to entertain doubts once we make up our minds is a subtle but deadly form of arrogance." With this advice in mind, Introducing Issues with Opposing Viewpoints books aim to open readers' minds to the critically divergent views that comprise our world's most important debates.

Introducing Issues with Opposing Viewpoints simplifies for students the enormous and often overwhelming mass of material now available via print and electronic media. Collected in every volume is an array of opinions that captures the essence of a particular controversy or topic. Introducing Issues with Opposing Viewpoints books embody the spirit of nineteenth-century journalist Charles A. Dana's axiom: "Fight for your opinions, but do not believe that they contain the whole truth, or the only truth." Absorbing such contrasting opinions teaches students to analyze the strength of an argument and compare it to its opposition. From this process readers can inform and strengthen their own opinions, or be exposed to new information that will change their minds. Introducing Issues with Opposing Viewpoints is a mosaic of different voices. The authors are statesmen, pundits, academics, journalists, corporations, and ordinary people who have felt compelled to share their experiences and ideas in a public forum. Their words have been collected from newspapers, journals, books, speeches, interviews, and the Internet, the fastest growing body of opinionated material in the world.

Introducing Issues with Opposing Viewpoints shares many of the well-known features of its critically acclaimed parent series, Opposing Viewpoints. The articles are presented in a pro/con format, allowing readers to absorb divergent perspectives side by side. Active reading questions preface each viewpoint, requiring the student to approach the material thoughtfully and carefully. Useful charts, graphs, and cartoons supplement each article. A thorough introduction provides readers with crucial background on an issue. An annotated bibliography points the reader toward articles, books, and websites that contain additional information on the topic. An appendix of organizations to contact contains a wide variety of charities, nonprofit organizations, political groups, and private enterprises that each hold a position on the issue at hand. Finally, a comprehensive index allows readers to locate content quickly and efficiently.

Introducing Issues with Opposing Viewpoints is also significantly different from Opposing Viewpoints. As the series title implies, its presentation will help introduce students to the concept of opposing viewpoints and learn to use this material to aid in critical writing and debate. The series' four-color, accessible format makes the books attractive and inviting to readers of all levels. In addition, each viewpoint has been carefully edited to maximize a reader's understanding of the content. Short but thorough viewpoints capture the essence of an argument. A substantial, thought-provoking essay question placed at the end of each viewpoint asks the student to further investigate the issues raised in the viewpoint, compare and contrast two authors' arguments, or consider how one might go about forming an opinion on the topic at hand. Each viewpoint contains sidebars that include at-a-glance information and handy statistics. A Facts About section located in the back of the book further supplies students with relevant facts and figures.

Following in the tradition of the Opposing Viewpoints series, Greenhaven Press continues to provide readers with invaluable exposure to the controversial issues that shape our world. As John Stuart Mill once wrote: "The only way in which a human being can make some approach to knowing the whole of a subject is by hearing what can be said about it by persons of every variety of opinion and studying all modes in which it can be looked at by every character of mind. No wise man ever acquired his wisdom in any mode but this." It is to this principle that Introducing Issues with Opposing Viewpoints books are dedicated.

Introduction

It is estimated that 99 percent of all species that have ever lived on earth have gone extinct. Some of these died out naturally, slowly, and individually, while others perished in one of five mass extinction events that wiped out the majority of life that existed on the planet at that time.

Scientists think the first mass extinction occurred about 440 million years ago during a time called the late Ordovician period. During this time, most of the planet's land masses were connected, forming one huge continent known as Gondwana. As Gondwana shifted toward the South Pole, temperatures dropped. Massive glaciers formed and sea levels changed. A 20-million-year-long ice age ensued, which killed off about 85 percent of all species. It took about 25 million years for the planet to again become repopulated with a diverse array of species—many of them entirely new.

Once the supercontinent Gondwana dislodged itself from the South Pole area, it drifted north. During this journey, parts of it split off, becoming North America, northern Europe, Russia, and Greenland. The planet's species were developing rapidly during this period, giving way to marine life with teeth and marine life with legs that began to venture from the seas onto land. Then, about 365 million years ago, another mass extinction occurred, this one at the end of what is called the Devonian period. What caused this mass extinction is not exactly clear to scientists. "It is probably, in fact, composed of a number of separate events—as many as seven—spread over about 25 million years,"[1] note researchers Ricard V. Solé and Mark Newman of the Santa Fe Institute. Like the first mass extinction, this one was probably also caused by changes to the earth's climate. Whatever happened, between 70 and 80 percent of all living species were killed off and it took the earth about 30 million years to recover.

The third and largest extinction event to date occurred about 245 million years ago, at the end of the Permian era. Scientists believe that as many as 96 percent of all marine species perished in this event. The effect on land species was significant too: more than 70 percent went extinct. These extinctions were also probably due to climate change. Temperature changes might have caused the ocean's circulation patterns to shift, dramatically altering its temperature and chemistry. In fact, the fossil record shows that during this period sea levels rose and the water had low levels of oxygen and high levels of carbon dioxide. Volcanic activity may have contributed to the changes, too.

The earth had just 37 million years to rebound before it was hit by yet another mass extinction event. This one occurred in the late Triassic period, about 208 million years ago. Solé and Newman say that this is probably the most poorly understood of all of the major extinctions. A wetter, warmer planet, along with extreme volcano activity and possibly an asteroid, seem to have contributed to this die-off, in which up to 80 percent of all species perished in two main waves.

But the fourth mass extinction gave way to the creation of a new species: the dinosaurs. These famous creatures developed and roamed the earth for several million years until they too were wiped out in the fifth mass extinction, which occurred about 65 million years ago, at the end of the Cretaceous era. This extinction is well known not just for the dinosaur extinctions but also because of the dramatic way it was believed to have happened: The extinction was likely due to a giant comet or meteorite that crashed into the earth in what is now eastern Mexico. The crash critically changed the living conditions on earth: it caused acid rain, massive firestorms, a spike and then a drop in temperature, and as much as 40 percent of all land areas became flooded. Seventy percent of species were wiped out.

Over the next 30 million years, life on earth recovered, and species bloomed once again. But today, scientists question whether another mass extinction is under way. A prominent paper released in March 2011 in the science journal *Nature* concluded that a sixth extinction is likely occurring. Researchers found that prior to the 1600s, when humans began to boom, just two mammal species went extinct every million years. But since that time, at least eighty, and possibly more, mammal species have gone extinct. This rate of extinction, the study's researchers conclude, could mean that another mass extinction might be under way. "It looks like modern extinction rates resemble mass extinction rates,"[2] says researcher Anthony Barnosky.

Conservationist and *Animal Planet* host Jeff Corwin paints an even more dire picture, reporting that an animal species goes extinct every twenty minutes. At this rate, about half of all living species will be gone by the end of the twenty-first century, he says. Even worse, unlike the first five mass extinctions, this extinction event is believed not to be the result of natural temperature fluctuations, shifting continents, or extraterrestrial bombardment but of human activity. "The causes of this mass die-off are many: overpopulation, loss of habitat, global warming, species exploitation," writes Corwin. "The list goes on, but it all points to us."[3]

Others, however, disagree that we are in the middle of a sixth mass extinction, pointing out that species extinction is a natural and acceptable phenomenon. Furthermore, the current extinction event, referred to as the Holocene extinction event, is suspected to have begun around 10,000 B.C., which is thousands of years before the onslaught of human activity that Corwin warns about began. In addition, scientists do not really know how many species exist, and thus people like Hank Campbell, creator of the online scientific community Science 2.0, say it is impossible to know, and thus panic about, how many species we are losing. "Since we don't know how many species there are now, or have ever been, if someone makes a model and claims tens of thousands of species are going extinct today, that sets off cultural alarms," says Campbell. "It's not science."[4] Patrick Moore, the cofounder of the conservation organization Greenpeace, agrees and suggests that species might adapt to their changing environment rather than going extinct. "The authors [of the *Nature* study] greatly underestimate the rate [at which] new species can evolve, especially when existing species are under stress,"[5] he says. Moore is one of several people who have suggested that dire predictions of mass extinction are the latest focus of environmental hysteria.

Indeed, the prospect of a mass extinction—especially one caused by human activity—is scary, even if it is unclear whether there is reason for such fear. Whether such an extinction is actually occurring, and what its causes and consequences might be, are just one of the topics debated in *Introducing Issues with Opposing Viewpoints: Endangered Species*. Students will consider arguments about whether and to what extent species are threatened, how climate change is affecting species, and how endangered species can be best protected. Carefully crafted guided reading questions and thought-provoking essay prompts encourage students to develop their own opinions on this increasingly important topic.

Notes

1. Ricard V. Solé and Mark Newman, "Extinctions and Biodiversity in the Fossil Record," in *The Earth System: Biological and Ecological Dimensions of Global Environmental Change*, vol. 2, Harold A. Mooney and Josep G. Canadell, eds. Chichester, UK: John Wiley & Sons, 2002, pp. 297–301. http://complex.upf.es/~ricard/EGECfinal.pdf.
2. Quoted in "World's Sixth Mass Extinction May Be Underway," *Independent* (London), March 7, 2011. www.independent.co.uk/environment/worlds-sixth-mass-extinction-may-be-underway-study-2234388.html.
3. Jeff Corwin, "The Sixth Extinction," *Los Angeles Times*, November 30, 2009. http://articles.latimes.com/2009/nov/30/opinion/la-oe-corwin30-2009nov30.
4. Hank Campbell, "I Wouldn't Worry About the Latest Mass Extinction Scare," Science 2.0, March 8, 2011. www.science20.com/science2.0/i_wouldnt_worry_about_latest_mass_extinction_scare-76989.
5. Quoted in Marc Morano, "Greenpeace Co-founder Slams Species Extinction Scare Study as Proof of How 'Peer-Review Process Has Become Corrupted,'" ClimateDepot, March 4, 2011. www.climatedepot.com/a/9996/Greenpeace-CoFounder-Slams-Species-Extinction-Scare-Study-as-proof-of-how-peerreview-process-has-become-corrupted-ndash-Study-greatly-underestimate-the-rate-new-species-can-evolve.

Chapter 1

Is Species Extinction a Serious Problem?

The intent of the International Union for Conservation of Nature's Red List is to highlight those species that are facing a high risk of global extinction.

Mass Species Extinction Is Imminent

Elizabeth Kolbert

"If current trends continue, by the end of this century as many as half of earth's species will be gone."

In the following viewpoint Elizabeth Kolbert argues that the planet is poised to experience a devastating mass extinction. She explains that fossil and geological records reveal that the planet has already experienced at least twenty mass extinctions, five of which have been notably devastating. Today, species and habitat loss is occurring at such a fast pace that Kolbert suggests a sixth devastating mass extinction is under way. Human activity is largely responsible for this and prior extinctions, she says. Kolbert warns that if humans make no effort to curb carbon dioxide emissions, ocean acidification, habitat loss, and other environmentally threatening activities, the earth may lose up to half its current species by the twenty-first century's end.

Since 1999 Kolbert has been a staff writer at *The New Yorker*, a renowned journal of culture and letters.

Elizabeth Kolbert, "The Sixth Extinction?," *The New Yorker*, vol. 85, no. 15, May 25, 2009, pp. 53–63. Copyright © 2009 *The New Yorker*. All rights reserved. Reproduced by permission.

AS YOU READ, CONSIDER THE FOLLOWING QUESTIONS:
1. What percentage of all species does Kolbert say were exterminated by the end-Cretaceous event?
2. What does the author say is the difference between background extinctions and mass extinctions?
3. According to Kolbert, what percentage of amphibians are threatened with extinction today? What percentage of mammals, birds, and reef-building corals?

Of the many species that have existed on earth—estimates run as high as fifty billion—more than ninety-nine per cent have disappeared. In the light of this, it is sometimes joked that all of life today amounts to little more than a rounding error.

Records of the missing can be found everywhere in the world, often in forms that are difficult to overlook. And yet extinction has been a much contested concept. Throughout the eighteenth century, even as extraordinary fossils were being unearthed and put on exhibit, the prevailing view was that species were fixed, created by God for all eternity. If the bones of a strange creature were found, it must mean that that creature was out there somewhere. . . .

A Mass Extinction Is Already Under Way

Over the past half-billion years, there have been at least twenty mass extinctions, when the diversity of life on earth has suddenly and dramatically contracted. Five of these—the so-called Big Five—were so devastating that they are usually put in their own category. The first took place during the late Ordovician period, nearly four hundred and fifty million years ago, when life was still confined mainly to water. Geological records indicate that more than eighty per cent of marine species died out. The fifth occurred at the end of the Cretaceous period, sixty-five million years ago. The end-Cretaceous event exterminated not just the dinosaurs but seventy-five per cent of all species on earth.

The significance of mass extinctions goes beyond the sheer number of organisms involved. In contrast to ordinary, or so-called background, extinctions, which claim species that, for one reason

Are We Due for Another Mass Extinction?

Extinctions are common in the geologic history of the earth. At least five mass extinctions have occurred, and some scientists believe a sixth is under way.

The Five Mass Extinctions in Earth's History

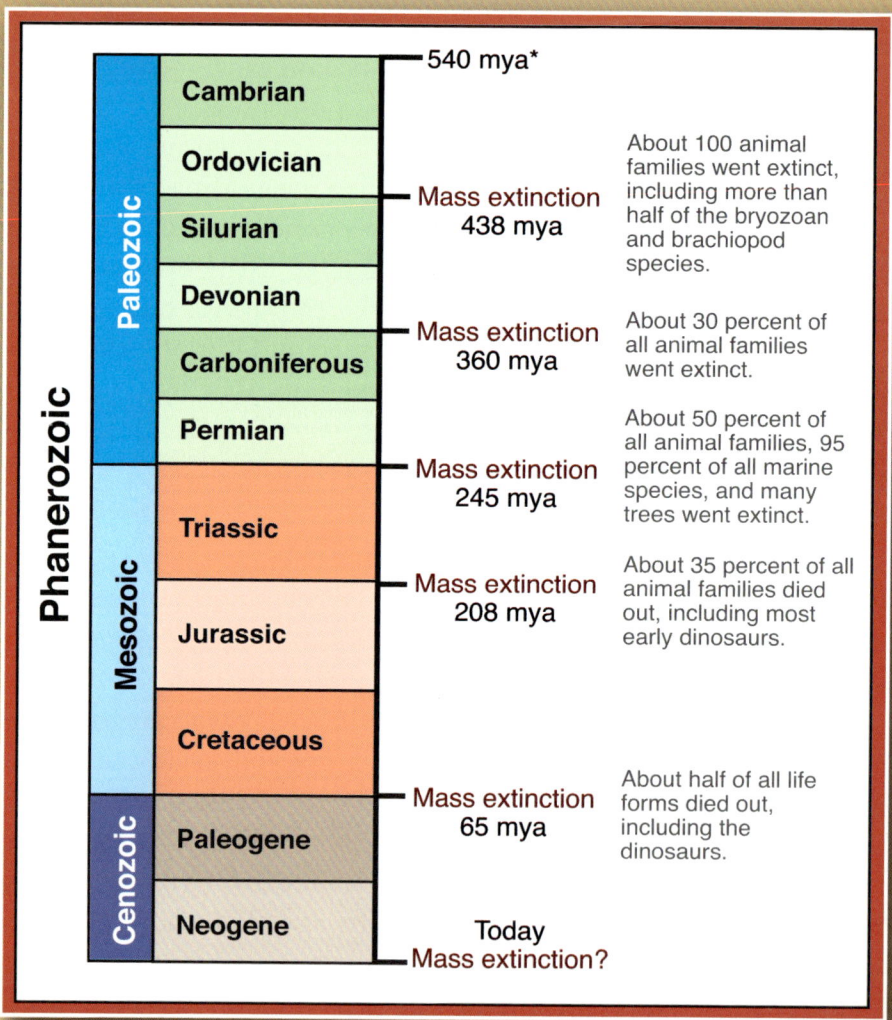

*millions of years ago (mya)

Taken from: National Aeronautics and Space Administration, 2010.

or another, have become unfit, mass extinctions strike down the fit and the unfit all at once. For example, brachiopods, which look like clams but have an entirely different anatomy, dominated the ocean floor for hundreds of millions of years. In the third of the Big Five extinctions—the end-Permian—the hugely successful brachiopods were nearly wiped out, along with trilobites, blastoids, and curypterids. (In the end-Permian event, more than ninety per cent of marine species and seventy per cent of terrestrial species vanished; the event is sometimes referred to as "the mother of mass extinctions" or "the great dying.")

Once a mass extinction occurs, it takes millions of years for life to recover, and when it does it generally has a new cast of characters; following the end-Cretaceous event, mammals rose up (or crept out) to replace the departed dinosaurs. In this way, mass extinctions, though missing from the original theory of evolution, have played a determining role in evolution's course; as [paleoanthropologist] Richard Leakey has put it, such events "restructure the biosphere" and so "create the pattern of life." It is now generally agreed among biologists that another mass extinction is under way. Though it's difficult to put a precise figure on the losses, it is estimated that, if current trends continue, by the end of this century as many as half of earth's species will be gone. . . .

It is difficult to say when, exactly, the current extinction event—sometimes called the sixth extinction—began. What might be thought of as its opening phase appears to have started about fifty thousand years ago. At that time, Australia was home to a fantastic assortment of enormous animals; these included a wombatlike creature the size of a hippo, a land tortoise nearly as big as a VW Beetle, and the giant short-faced kangaroo, which grew to be ten feet tall. Then all of the continent's largest animals disappeared. Every species of marsupial weighing more than two hundred pounds—there were nineteen of them—vanished, as did three species of giant reptiles and a flightless bird with stumpy legs known as *Genyornis newtoni*.

Humans Contribute to Mass Extinction Events

This die-off roughly coincided with the arrival of the first people on the continent, probably from Southeast Asia. Australia is a big place, and there couldn't have been very many early settlers. For a long time, the coincidence was discounted. Yet, thanks to recent work by geologists and paleontologists, a clear global pattern has emerged. About eleven thousand years ago, three-quarters of North America's largest animals—among them mastodons, mammoths, giant beavers, short-faced bears, and sabre-toothed tigers—began to go extinct. This is right around the time the first humans are believed to have wandered onto the continent across the Bering land bridge. In relatively short order, the first humans settled South America as well. Subsequently, more than thirty species of South American "megamammals," including elephant-size ground sloths and rhinolike creatures known as toxodons, died out.

And what goes for Australia and the Americas also goes for many other parts of the world. Humans settled Madagascar around two thousand years ago; the island subsequently lost all mammals weighing more than twenty pounds, including pygmy hippos and giant lemurs.

"Substantial losses have occurred throughout near time," Ross MacPhee, a curator at the American Museum of Natural History, in New York, and an expert on extinctions of the recent geological past, has written. "In the majority of cases, these losses occurred when, and only when, people began to expand across areas that had never before experienced their presence." The Maori arrived in New Zealand around eight hundred years ago. They encountered eleven species of moas—huge ostrichlike creatures without wings. Within a few centuries—and possibly within a single century—all eleven moa species were gone. While these "first contact" extinctions were most pronounced among large animals, they were not confined to them. Humans discovered the Hawaiian Islands

> **FAST FACT**
>
> According to an October 2010 study by the International Union for the Conservation of Nature (IUCN), 33 percent of fishes, 33 percent of coral reef species, 25 percent of mammals, 22 percent of reptiles, and 13 percent of birds are threatened with extinction. The IUCN reports that 41 percent of the world's amphibians face extinction, and 120 amphibian species have vanished entirely in the past three decades.

around fifteen hundred years ago; soon afterward, ninety per cent of Hawaii's native bird species disappeared.

"We expect extinction after people arrive on an island," David Steadman, the curator of ornithology at the Florida Museum of Natural History, has written. "Survival is the exception."

The Quick and Deadly Nature of Human Activity

Why was first contact with humans so catastrophic? Some of the animals may have been hunted to death; thousands of moa bones have been found at Maori archeological sites, and man-made artifacts have been uncovered near mammoth and mastodon remains at more than a dozen sites in North America. Hunting, however, seems insufficient to account for so many losses across so many different taxa in so many parts of the globe. A few years ago, researchers analyzed hundreds of bits of emu and *Genyornis newtoni* eggshell, some dating from long before the first people arrived in Australia and some from after. They found that around forty-five thousand years ago, rather abruptly, emus went from eating all sorts of plants to relying mainly on shrubs. The researchers hypothesized that Australia's early settlers periodically set the countryside on fire—perhaps to flush out prey—a practice that would have reduced the variety of plant life. Those animals which, like emus, could cope with a changed landscape survived, while those which, like *Genyornis*, could not died out. . . .

In the end, the most deadly aspect of human activity may simply be the pace of it. Just in the past century, CO_2 levels in the atmosphere have changed by as much—a hundred parts per million—as they normally do in a hundred-thousand-year glacial cycle. Meanwhile, the drop in ocean pH levels that has occurred over the past fifty years may well exceed anything that happened in the seas during the previous fifty million. In a single afternoon, a pathogen like Bd[1] can move, via United or American Airlines, halfway around the world. Before man entered the picture, such a migration would have required hundreds, if not thousands, of years—if, indeed, it could have been completed at all.

---

1. *Batrachochytrium dendrobatidis*, a microorganism that attacks amphibians.

This Permian sea life diorama depicts sponges, corals, cephalopods, and brachiopods on the ocean floor. The mass extinction at the end of the Permian period has been called "the mother of mass extinctions"—according to the author, more than 90 percent of marine life was wiped out.

"The Stress Is Us"

Currently, a third of all amphibian species, nearly a third of reef-building corals, a quarter of all mammals, and an eighth of all birds are classified as "threatened with extinction." These estimates do not include the species that humans have already wiped out or the species for which there are insufficient data. Nor do the figures take into account the projected effects of global warming or ocean acidification. Nor, of course, can they anticipate the kinds of sudden, terrible collapses that are becoming almost routine.

I asked [Harvard paleontolgist Andrew] Knoll to compare the current situation with past extinction events. He told me that he didn't want to exaggerate recent losses, or to suggest that an extinction on the order of the end-Cretaceous or end-Permian was imminent. At

18   Endangered Species

the same time, he noted, when the asteroid hit the Yucatán "it was one terrible afternoon." He went on, "But it was a short-term event, and then things started getting better. Today, it's not like you have a stress and the stress is relieved and recovery starts. It gets bad and then it keeps being bad, because the stress doesn't go away. Because the stress is us."

> **EVALUATING THE AUTHOR'S ARGUMENTS:**
>
> Elizabeth Kolbert warns that as many as 50 percent of the planet's species may be extinct by the century's end. What would Stephen Budiansky, author of the following viewpoint, say about the accuracy of this number? Quote from both viewpoints in your answer, and then state with which author you ultimately agree and why.

Viewpoint 2

Predictions of Mass Extinction Are Unfounded

Stephen Budiansky

"Wholly unsubstantiated predictions of catastrophic mass extinctions [are] only undermining the credibility of environmentalists."

It is impossible to make accurate predictions about mass extinction argues Stephen Budiansky in the following viewpoint. He discusses a formula that environmentalists have used to make dire and scary predictions about extinctions. According to Budiansky, this formula is scientifically inaccurate and does not conform to environmental realities. For example, according to the formula, forest loss in the United States should have caused about thirty bird extinctions; Budiansky says that, in reality, it only caused two. He concludes that those who warn of mass extinctions are using bad science to sell panic and ruining the credibility of environmentalists in the process.

Budiansky writes about science and history and is the author of *The Covenant of the Wild: Why Animals Chose Domestication* (1999).

Stephen Budiansky, "The Teflon Doomsayers," Stephen Budiansky's Liberal Curmudgeon Blog, September 26, 2010. http://budiansky.blogspot.com/2010/09/teflon-doomsayers.html. Reproduced by permission of Stephen Budiansky.

AS YOU READ, CONSIDER THE FOLLOWING QUESTIONS:
1. What does Budiansky mean when he says "save the whales" is a better fund-raising tool than "the whales are being saved"?
2. Who is Norman Myers and how does he factor into the author's argument?
3. What does Budiansky say happened to Brazilian species when more than 90 percent of Brazil's Atlantic coastal forests were cut down?

In *The Rational Optimist*, [author] Matt Ridley offers example after spectacular example of a phenomenon that has baffled me ever since I began covering environmental issues in my first job in journalism thirty years ago: to wit, that while the entire presumable goal, purpose, and raison d'être [reason for being] of applied environmental science is to solve environmental problems, any environmental scientist who dares to suggest that problems *are* being solved is asking for trouble. As Ridley observes, we have arrived at a state where even the most wildly irrational pessimism is treated with reverence, while the most cautiously sober optimism is ridiculed. . . .

Pessimism is what people with deep minds and deep souls have; optimism is what idiots with vacant grins on their faces have.

It Pays to Be a Doomsayer

Pessimism is of course a proven fund-raising tool; "save the whales!" is always going to bring in more cash than "the whales are being saved!" But much more than that, we have today the amusingly ironic spectacle of tenured professors with salaries, health insurance, lifetime job security, and excellent retirement plans courtesy of [financial services company] TIAA-CREF being showered with worldly rewards (bestselling books, "genius" awards) for telling us that progress is an illusion and the end is near . . . while still preening themselves as daring outsiders courageously taking on the mighty and powerful. The fact that it takes no daring at all to adopt such an intellectual posture these days does not stop any of the practitioners of this business model from invariably announcing themselves to be the bearers of "dangerous" or "heretical" ideas and congratulating themselves for "speaking truth to power."

So there are understandable reasons why it pays to say that things have gone to hell and will continue to go to hell.

What I find almost inexplicable in all of this, however, is how the scientific doomsayers get away over and over again with making predictions that are fabulously, ridiculously—and demonstrably—incorrect, without the slightest repercussions upon their credibility or careers. Predictions of impending doom are published based on absurd methodologies and threadbare evidence of a kind that in the normal course of scientific affairs would be sufficient to ruin careers ten times over, and the authors walk away from them without a scratch. . . .

Predictions of Mass Extinction Are Baseless

The astonishingly wrong and repercussion-free prediction of imminent doom that first riveted my attention was the claim of the impending mass extinction of the Earth's species. In 1979, the biologist Norman Myers declared that a fifth of all species on the planet would be gone within two decades. This prediction was based upon . . . absolutely no evidence whatsoever. Myers acknowledged that the documented species extinction rate of animals was 1 per year; he then asserted that scientists had "hazarded a guess" that the actual rate was 100 per year; he then speculated that government inaction was "likely to lead" to several thousand or even tens of thousands a year, which would add up to as much as a million species over two decades. (This was when people thought there were 5 million species [living on the planet]; the best guess now is at least 10 million.) It swiftly became conventional wisdom.

Subsequently, an attempt was made to give these made-up numbers a patina of scientific respectability that was in many ways an even worse abuse of scientific logic and evidence. In the 1990s [biologist] E.O. Wilson began citing the so-called "species-area relation" as the basis for predicting that tens of thousands of species were being extirpated a year by habitat loss caused by forest clearing. Wilson popularized various numbers ranging from 4,000 to 100,000 species a year being lost, and these numbers were repeated over and over again in environmental groups' fundraising literature, in congressional testimony, [and] in speeches by [former US vice president and now environmentalist] Al Gore (who in 1993 said that "one-half of all species" could disappear in our lifetime, apparently an extrapolation

"Frogs Concerned About Humans," cartoon by Chris Slane, PoliticalCartoons.com, February 1, 2005. Copyright © 2005 Chris Slane, New Zealand, and PoliticalCartoons.com. All rights reserved.

of Wilson's and [scientist Paul] Ehrlich's pronouncement, in a 1991 paper in *Science*, that as many as a quarter of all rain forest species will disappear in 30 years).

A "Cockamamie" Formula

I started to look into the science and mathematics of the species-area relation when my father, who was an applied mathematician at Harvard University, mentioned to me an Op-ed in the *New York Times* by his fellow Harvard faculty member Wilson that included a description of this formula, which had struck my father as absurd on its face as a mathematical model. The formula most often used is:

$$S = CA^z$$

where S is number of species, A is area, and C and z are arbitrary constants tweaked to make the curve try to match the data. Basically, the formula says if you count the number of species on, say, islands of varying sizes, the bigger the island, the more the species. Wilson's argument was that if you start cutting down rain forests, say, you'll shrink the number of species contained in them according to the same curve.

The prima facie [at first sight] problem, which irked my father, is that the dimensions of the arbitrary constant C vary according to the numerical value of the other arbitrary constant z. Without going into the technical details too much, this is (as my father put it) "cockamamie" from any scientific perspective; it means that this is just an exercise in curve-fitting, not a scientific model based on any cause-and-effect understanding or mechanism.

No Biological Significance to Extinction Formula

The more I looked into it the more ridiculous it became. The definitive review article on the species-area relation correctly noted that the formula is at heart nothing more than a "sampling phenomenon . . . without a functional relationship." The authors concluded that there was no biological significance to the constants C and z; the fact that z tends to fall in the range of 0.2 to 0.4 when you fit the curve to islands is simply a mathematical coincidence, and the same thing happens when the same formula is used to fit other empirical relationships (e.g., the relation between brain size and body size in mammals).

The much more serious problem, as a few (truly daring) conservation biologists pointed out, is that there is absolutely no reason to think that such an empirical, broad-brush, descriptive formula has any predictive value in the real world at all. As the conservation biologist Vernon Heywood wrote: "The species-area curve (in a mainland situation) is nothing more than a self-evident fact: that as one enlarges an area, it comes to encompass the geographical ranges of more species. The danger comes when this is extrapolated backwards, and it is assumed that by reducing the size of a forest, it will lose species according to the same gradient."

> **FAST FACT**
>
> University of Queensland (Australia) researchers Diana Fisher and Simon Blomberg reported in September 2010 that at least 67 of the 187 mammal species that have been classified as extinct, extinct in the wild, or probably extinct since 1500 have been rediscovered.

A satellite image shows the effects of deforestation in the Amazon Basin and the Atlantic coastal forests of Brazil. Although 90 percent of the coastal forests have been cut down, no indigenous species are known to have become extinct as a result.

Species Do Not Follow Formula Rules

Heywood pointed out many reasons why this is not going to happen: species are not distributed at random, conservation measures are already protecting many critical habitats, [and] many species can adapt to other habitats as the original forests are cut down. Rather than seeing species numbers decline in lockstep with loss of forest area, a more biologically realistic model might predict few if any extinctions until habitats are almost completely destroyed, and even then species numbers would certainly not plunge to zero (as the species-area curve predicts), since many species would be able to survive in the secondary forests that regrow or in other habitats still available.

Even more striking is the fact that the predictions from the formula are wildly incorrect in practice where they can be checked. More than 90 percent of the Atlantic coastal forests of Brazil were cut down, mostly in the 19th century; by the species-area relation that means 50 percent of species should be gone. In fact the actual number of animal extinctions has been *zero*, even though many of the Brazilian species are highly endemic, found nowhere else in the world.

Similarly, the eastern U.S. forests were reduced to less than half their original extent from colonial times to 1900; but instead of 30 extinctions of birds as predicted by the model, there have been 4—2 of which (the Carolina parakeet and the passenger pigeon) were wiped out by hunting, not habitat loss, and the other 2 of which (the ivory-billed woodpecker and Bachman's warbler) were restricted to very specific habitats in the southeast that were destroyed by logging and agriculture. The fact is you could have cut down vastly more forest area in the entire region east of the Rockies without losing a single bird species had we protected the small but critical habitats required by the ivory-billed woodpecker and Bachman's warbler and halted the criminally stupid hunting of the passenger pigeon and Carolina parakcct. (Please note: I am not advocating cutting down vast areas of forest east of the Rockies.) . . .

Stop Using Bad Science to Sell Panic

There is no scientific dispute that extinctions are occurring, that they are occurring at a rate above the natural level due to human action, and that strenuous efforts are needed to protect critical habitats, to eliminate invasive competitors that threaten species, and to prevent overexploitation.

But the egregiously bad science that is still being invoked to shore up wholly unsubstantiated predictions of catastrophic mass extinctions is only undermining the credibility of environmentalists, and is already causing a dangerous political backlash that has handed ammunition (exactly as in the case of global warming) to those who want to reject any and all evidence of human impacts on the natural environment.

A first step in restoring credibility might be to revive some intellectual opprobrium for those who are flagrantly wrong, even in a good cause.

EVALUATING THE AUTHOR'S ARGUMENTS:

Stephen Budiansky says a profitable industry has sprung up from environmental doomsaying. What do you think—do you agree that the environmental movement has profited from sounding alarms over environmental issues like mass extinction? Or do you think that this is too cynical a position to take and that those who warn of environmental disaster are truly trying to protect the planet? Explain your position.

Viewpoint 3

Biodiversity Loss Has Disastrous Consequences for Humankind

Richard Conniff

"We need to understand in short that our lives depend on species most of us have never heard of."

In the following viewpoint Richard Conniff argues that biodiversity—the rich variety of species on earth—is essential to the health and prosperity of humans. He discusses how numerous medicines, including treatments for cancer and diabetes, are derived from a rich array of plant, animal, and microbial species. Without these species, humans would not only lack medicinal cures, they would also have less oxygen to breathe and be vulnerable to environmental chaos. Conniff says it is ironic that billions of dollars are spent trying to explore microbes in space when a vast array of species are awaiting discovery on earth. He concludes that until the value of every species is fully understood, humans must take pains to protect them all.

Conniff is the author of six books, including *The Natural History of the Rich: A Field*

Richard Conniff, "What Are Species Worth? Putting a Price on Biodiversity," in *Yale Environment 360*, September 27, 2010. Copyright © 2010. Reproduced by permission of the author.

Guide and *The Species Seekers: Heroes, Fools, and the Mad Pursuit of Life on Earth*. His articles have been published in *Time, Smithsonian, The Atlantic, National Geographic,* and *Yale Environment 360*.

AS YOU READ, CONSIDER THE FOLLOWING QUESTIONS:
1. What is *Prochlorococcus* and how does it factor into the author's argument?
2. What is taxol, and where does the author say it comes from?
3. What use has been found for gila monster venom, according to Conniff?

We live in what is paradoxically a great age of discovery and also of mass extinction. Astonishing new species turn up daily, as new roads and new technologies penetrate formerly remote habitats. And species also vanish forever, at what scientists estimate to be 100 to 1,000 times the normal rate of extinction.

The Importance of Species

Over the past few years, as I was working on a book about the history of species discovery, I often found myself coming back to a fundamental question: Why do species matter? That is, why should ordinary people care if scientists discover one species or pronounce the demise of another?

It may seem too obvious to need asking. In certain limited contexts, people clearly do care. We will go to great lengths to protect a boutique species like the giant panda, for instance. We also thrill to the possibility of finding the slightest microbial hint of life in outer space, hardly blinking when the U.S. government spends $7 billion a year largely for that purpose. Meanwhile, we spend pennies exploring the alien life forms that are all around us here on Earth.

Maybe it's just human nature not to value—or even see—the thing that's right in front of our faces. And maybe it's also a failure of communication. That is, scientists may need to explain their work on a far more basic level—not "Why do species matter?" but "Is food important to you?" or "Do you want your children to have effective medicines when they get sick?" or even "Do you like to breathe?" None of these questions overstates the importance of species.

Many Species Have Been Forever Lost

In 2008 almost one in four mammals were at risk of disappearing forever, according to the IUCN Red List of Threatened Species (IUCN 2008). The IUCN also reports that at least seventy-six mammal species and seven mammal subspecies have become extinct since the year 1500 (IUCN 2010).

Species of mammals that recently became globally extinct include:

Nullarbor Dwarf Bettong	Little Swan Island Hutia
Oriente Cave Rat	Insular Cave Rat
Torre's Cave Rat	Imposter Hutia
Bory's White Bat	Madagascan Dwarf Hippopotamus
Aurochs	
Hispaniolan Edible Rat	Malagasy Hippo
Desert Rat Kangaroo	Bluebuck
Giant Canary Island Rat	Steller's Sea Cow
Pig-footed Bandicoot	Montane Hutia
White-footed Rabbit-Rat	Puerto Rican Hutia
Buhler's Rat	Candango Mouse
Red-bellied Gracile Mouse Opossum	Central Hare-Wallaby
	Eastern Hare-Wallaby
Giant Fossa	Peruvian Viscacha
Machu Picchu Chinchilla Rat	Toolache Wallaby
Giant Vampire Bat	Lesser Bilby
Falkland Island Wolf	Lava Mouse
Red Gazelle	Antillean Giant Rice Rat
Arabian Gazelle	Santa Lucia Giant Rice Rat
Queen of Sheba's Gazelle	Galapágos Giant Rat
Saudi Gazelle	Caribbean Monk Seal
Cuban Coney	Anthony's Woodrat

Bunkers Woodrat	Desert Bandicoot
San Martin Island Woodrat	Pemberton's Deer Mouse
Sea Mink	Samana Hutia
Puerto Rican Nesophontes	Broad-Faced Potoroo
Atalaye Nesophontes	Sardinian Pika
Greater Cuban Nesophontes	Blue-Grey Mouse
Western Cuban Nesophontes	Gould's Mouse
Saint Michel Nesophontes	Dusky Flying Fox
Haitian Nesophontes	Large Palau Flying Fox
Darwin's Galapagos Mouse	Lesser Mascarene Flying Fox
Indefatigable Galapagos Mouse	Guam Flying Fox
Vespucci's Rodent	Puerto Rican Flower Bat
Short-Tailed Hopping-Mouse	Twisted-Toothed Mouse
Long-Tailed Hopping-Mouse	Maclear's Rat
Big-Eared Hopping-Mouse	Bulldog Rat
Darling Downs Hopping-Mouse	Schomburgk's Deer
Nendo Tube-Nosed Fruit Bat	Lemke's Hutia
St. Vincent Pygmy Rice Rat	Marcano's Solenodon
Crescent Nailtail Wallaby	Tasmanian Tiger
Jamaican Rice Rat	Jamaican Monkey
Nelson's Rice Rat	Japanese Sea Lion
Large Sloth Lemur	

Taken from: P.H.J. Maas, The Sixth Edition.com, TSEW (2011), February 2011. www.petermaas.nl/extinct/listsmammals.htm.

For instance, *Prochlorococcus* is an ocean-dwelling genus of cyanobacteria and among the most abundant life forms on Earth. Why should we care? Because it produces about 20 percent of the oxygen we breathe—and yet until an MIT [Massachusetts Institute of Technology] microbiologist named Sally Chisholm discovered it in 1986, *Prochlorococcus* was unknown. We need to understand in short that our lives depend on species most of us have never heard of—species we otherwise tend to shrug off as obscure, trivial, even undesirable.

We Rely on Species to Perform "Ecosystem Services"

Vultures, for instance. When we cause a species to go into decline, we almost never know—and hardly even stop to think about—what we might be losing in the process. In truth, it may be hard to think about, because the cascading effects of our actions are sometimes freakishly distant from the original cause. So in India in the early 1990s, farmers began using the anti-inflammatory drug diclofenac for the apparently worthy purpose of relieving pain and fever in their livestock. Unfortunately, vultures scavenging on livestock carcasses accumulated large quantities of the drug and promptly died of renal failure. Over a 14-year period, populations of three vulture species plummeted by between 96.8 and 99.9 percent.

Losing these efficient scavengers meant livestock carcasses often got left in the open to rot. It was one of those "ecosystem services"—manufacturing oxygen, soaking up carbon dioxide, preventing floods, taking out the garbage—that species generally provide unnoticed, until they stop. But the impacts went well beyond the stench, according to a 2008 article in *Ecological Economics*. Moving into the niche vacated by the vultures, feral dog populations boomed by up to 9 million animals over the same period. Dog bites and the incidence of rabies in humans also increased, and the authors conservatively estimated that an additional 48,000 people died during the 14-year period as a result. Calculating the bottom-line worth of what we get from the natural world is notoriously difficult. But even pricing lives at a fraction of developed world values, the near-total loss of three insignificant vulture species has so far cost India an estimated $24 billion. . . .

Millions of Species Have Untapped Value

So do individual species matter? Or is it just the diversity of species? The truth is that our understanding of the natural world is far too primitive for anyone to say one species is important, and another isn't. In fact, scientists don't even have names for most species; they've described only about 1.8 million of them, with an estimated 10 to 50 million still to go. So instead of waging pitched battles for individual species, conservationists in recent years have prudently tended to emphasize diversity, working to protect large swaths of habitat for a multitude of species. It's the motorcycle mechanic's approach to conservation, as articulated by [ecologist] Aldo Leopold: "To keep every cog and wheel is the first precaution of intelligent tinkering."

But that should not stop us from trumpeting the benefits to humanity from individual species that might otherwise get written off as worthless, or even as impediments to human progress. Some conservationists may cringe at the thought of cheapening the natural world by defending it in economic terms. But NASA [National Aeronautics and Space Administration] manages to hold onto a sense of wonder about its mission while simultaneously touting the idea that space exploration can pay for itself in technology transfers to the civilian world. (There's actually a NASA "spinoff coloring book." It celebrates an outer space mirror-polishing technology now also used to make ice skates go "super fast!") The difference is that the spinoff argument for exploring species here on Earth is far more persuasive.

> **FAST FACT**
>
> Biodiversity loss means the loss of potential wonder drugs for the treatment of human illness. For example, the endangered Pacific yew tree is the source of the ovarian and breast cancer drug Taxol. The endangered waxy monkey frog of South America, which secretes dermaseptin, is used to treat antibiotic-resistant staphylococcus infections.

Life-Saving Medicines Came from Species

The yew, for instance, was until recently a "trash tree," says David J. Newman of the National Cancer Institute; he figures it was last valued

A Taiwanese silviculture specialist shows the size to which his biotech Yew trees will grow. Yew trees produce the key ingredient in Taxol, a drug used in treating cancer.

around the time his ancestors used it to fashion bows for firing arrows at the Battle of Agincourt. But it's now the source for taxol, relied on by tens of thousands of people as a life-saving treatment for breast, prostate, and ovarian cancers. Sales topped $1.6 billion last year [2009], according to IMS Health, a healthcare information and consulting company. Likewise, no one ever marched to save the gila monsters, but their venom is the source of a new drug for people who resist conventional treatments for Type 2 diabetes, an epidemic disease now on track to affect more than a third of all Americans over their lifetimes.

In fact, the common idea that drug companies can cook up their medicines out of thin air through "rational drug design" in the laboratory is simply wrong. One recent study looked at more than 1,000 drugs approved worldwide over a 20-year period and found not one that was traceable to a totally synthetic source. Getting our ideas from species in the natural world is still the rule.

Likewise, wild species continue to be the mother lode of genetic material for making agricultural crops more productive, or more resistant to pests, disease, and drought. That kind of bio-prospecting is likely to become far more important over the next few years as biologists begin to explore the bacteria, fungi, and other microbial life forms that help plants do what they do. In fact, we will have little choice but to find smarter ways of exploiting the hidden resources of the natural world. If NASA in its glory years had a mission—to get to the moon in 10 years—biologists now have one, too: To sustain the species and habitat here on Earth that will be essential to providing food, medicine, and sanity as the human population grows to 9 billion people over the next 40 years.

Biodiversity Offers Beauty and Delight

There is one final argument for the value of species, and it has to do with beauty, biophilia, and a sense of the sacred. In the course of researching my book on species discovery, it seemed to me that one young 19th-century specialist in marine mollusks made the case most persuasively. In pursuit of new species along the coast of Alaska, naturalist William T. Dall experienced all the usual adventures, among them a long frigid trip in a sealskin dory across open water, trying to avoid being crushed by waves loaded with cakes of ice.

He gave his family an eloquent explanation of what motivated him, and by extrapolation most other species seekers: "There is a singular delight," he wrote home in 1866, "in taking these delicate and almost microscopic animals and putting them under a strong glass, seeing the tiny heart beat, and blood circulate and gills expand, counting the muscles and blood vessels and almost the tiny disks that form the blood and to know that you are the first that has penetrated these mysteries and are perhaps the only one who ever will, and that all your notes and drawings and observations are so much solid knowledge added to the power and grace and beauty of the Infinite."

EVALUATING THE AUTHOR'S ARGUMENTS:

To make his argument, Richard Conniff cites the example of how the death of vultures in India led to an increase in rotting livestock carcasses, a boom in wild dog populations, increased rabies cases, more than ten thousand deaths, and $24 billion in losses. Did this example convince you of the importance of biodiversity? Why or why not?

Viewpoint 4

The Threat of Biodiversity Loss Is Exaggerated

Doug L. Hoffman

"It is hard to make definitive statements regarding loss of diversity when science cannot even tell us how many different creatures there are on the planet."

In the following viewpoint Doug L. Hoffman rejects claims that the planet's biodiversity is under threat. He points out that scientists have no idea exactly how many species exist. Therefore, it is impossible for them to say with any degree of accuracy that a catastrophic number of them are disappearing. In Hoffman's opinion, there are several signs that biodiversity is not under threat. Among these are the decline in deforestation and loss of habitat; the boom of protected species populations; and shaky science that tends to favor hysterical thinking. He concludes that the threat of biodiversity loss is exaggerated and people should reject claims of a biodiversity crisis.

Hoffman has worked as a mathematician, a computer programmer, an engineer, a computer salesman, a scientist, and a college professor. He is coauthor of the book *The Resilient Earth* and its companion website, which offer a skeptical perspective on science, energy, and environmental topics.

Doug L. Hoffman, "Biodiversity: Manufacturing a Crisis," www.theresilientearth.com, October 3, 2010. Reproduced by permission of the author.

AS YOU READ, CONSIDER THE FOLLOWING QUESTIONS:
1. What measures does Hoffman say have helped reverse the problem of deforestation?
2. What protected animal has killed hundreds of Tanzanians, according to Hoffman?
3. Why are some animals being poisoned in Africa, according to the author?

With the UN trying to promote diminishing biodiversity as the NEXT BIG CRISIS it is interesting to note the chaos among diversity researchers. It is hard to make definitive statements regarding loss of diversity when science cannot even tell us how many different creatures there are on the planet. Nevertheless, the UN has launched the *International Year of Biodiversity*, warning that the ongoing loss of species around the world is affecting human well-being. Yet another UN generated "science based" crisis to keep the world's citizens in a frenzy—shades of the failed global warming crisis, which the UN is rather hoping we all will forget.

A "Crisis" of Unknowable Proportion

In the July 2, 2010, issue of *Science*, Robert M. May from the Zoology Department, University of Oxford, offered a perspective on Earth's species count. In "Tropical Arthropod Species, More or Less?" May notes that scientists began systematically naming species just a little over two centuries ago. His best estimate is 1.6 to 1.7 million, with an additional 15,000 new species identified each year. Here is how he opened his article:

> If some alien version of the Starship Enterprise visited Earth, what might be the visitors' first question? I think it would be: "How many distinct life forms—species—does your planet have?" Embarrassingly, our best-guess answer would be in the range of 5 to 10 million eukaryotes (never mind the viruses and bacteria), but we could defend numbers exceeding 100 million, or as low as 3 million.

Eukaryotes have cells with a defined nucleus containing genetic material and include all complex forms of multicellular life. May suggests "it makes sense to begin an estimate of global arthropod species numbers by focusing on tropical beetles, partly because tropical arthropods dominate the global total, and partly because beetle species are both functionally diverse and represent roughly one-third of all arthropods." He then goes on to issue some other scientific guesstimates. But his attempt at clarifying the situation did not set well with all taxonomists [scientists who classify species].

Jaboury Ghazoul, of the Department of Environmental Sciences, ETH Zurich [a large, renowned science and technology university], is demanding a recount. In a letter published in the September 24 issue of *Science,* Ghazoul suggests that May has got his sums wrong and has only contributed to further confusion. Ghazoul concludes that science needs greater "rigor" to avoid carelessness. Here is his rebuttal to May's article:

> If aliens visited earth, perhaps they would wonder how many distinct life forms our planet has. With their advanced intellect and technology, they might well have the answer. It is clear from R.M. May's Perspective "Tropical arthropod species, more or less?" (2 July, p. 41) that we do not. May inadvertently adds to the confusion by indicating that New Guinea is home to roughly one-third of tropical tree species. Given that about 6000 tropical tree species are from New Guinea out of 37,000 tree species in all rainforests, only about 16% of tropical tree species are from this region—about half the estimate provided by May.

Forests Are Being Preserved

Once again the truth has slipped out—science has no idea how many species share the planet with us. Not how many arthropods (animals with exoskeletons, including insects, arachnids, and crustaceans), not how many tropical trees, not how many simple bacteria. Yet the UN in its various guises has been clamoring about a "crisis" in biodiversity. This notwithstanding good news on several fronts including a report from the UN Food and Agriculture Organization (FAO) that finds deforestation has diminished over the past decade.

According to the document, entitled "Global Forest Resources Assessment 2010," forest loss rates are highest in Africa and South America, where methods of controlling the phenomenon are lacking. Even so, the global average deforestation rate is going down. Reportedly, this is not due to more people becoming aware of the importance of forests, but to the fact that China has been planting enormous amounts of new trees yearly. Additionally, Brazil and Indonesia have been implementing programs to preserve their rain forests, punishing those who cut down trees illegally. . . .

Protected Animals Are Thriving

So the biodiversity debate muddles on—over fish, forests and other wildlife. Wolves reintroduced to areas around the Great Lakes and Yellowstone National Park are doing so well that the government wants to shoot some of them. A number of naturalists blame the decline of elk in the Rocky Mountain states on predation by wolves, and Alaskan wolves are reportedly killing an inordinate number of

A Texas-born panther is released in the Florida Everglades. Panther populations have increaed due to conservation efforts.

young moose. A US District judge ruled against the Alaska Fish and Game Department in their desire to kill seven wolves on Unimak Island, even though the wolves have reduced the island's caribou herd from 1,200 to fewer than 400.

In Florida, concern over inbreeding among the indigenous Florida panther led scientists to introduce 8 breeding females from Texas. "Big cats may be popular in places where they've become scarce and most people live in cities, but the rest of the world still struggles to deal with the dangers that man-eaters and cattle-killers pose to rural residents," states the perspective by [ecology professor] Craig Packer.

"Lions attacked more than 100 Tanzanians every year for the first few years of this millennium, and thousands of livestock are killed by lions, leopards, and jaguars throughout the world each year."

> **FAST FACT**
> *Reason* science writer Ronald Bailey reports that in New Zealand, nineteenth-century European settlers introduced two thousand new plant species. Since then only three of New Zealand's two thousand native species have gone extinct.

The vigor of individual panthers and the size of the Florida panther population have both increased since the Texas relocation. But more panthers means more incidents between humans and the big cats, who can reach a weight of 170 lbs (80 kg). It remains to be seen how the public will react to increased pet and livestock deaths, let alone any attacks on humans. Panthers lose some of their appeal when they have just made a meal out of little Fluffy or little Susie.

Several American states have raised their yearly trophy hunting limits for panthers (called pumas or cougars in other locations). In Africa, retaliatory poisoning is increasing outside of national parks and protected areas. It would seem that there is ongoing conflict between environmentalists' efforts to preserve biodiversity and humans exercising their fundamental rights as animals—protection of life and territory.

Hysteria over Biodiversity Loss Is Unwarranted

Lack of proper science, contradictory claims by activists and experts, conflicts with the needs of average people just trying to live their

Americans Are Not Concerned About Species Loss

A poll by *Newsweek* magazine found that Americans think global warming, water pollution, and air pollution are all greater environmental problems than the loss of endangered species.

Question: "Which one of the following do you think is the most important environmental problem facing the world today?"

Problem	Percentage
Global Warming	38
Water Pollution	14
Air Pollution	13
Garbage and Landfills	10
Loss of Ozone Layer	7
Endangered or Vanished Species	3
Acid Rain	1
Other/Unsure	7/7

Taken from: *Newsweek* poll, August 1–2, 2007. www.consequencesofglobalwarming.com/polls.

lives—yes, this sounds like a UN generated, politically motivated "crisis." After all, the bureaucrats and parasites at the UN rode the global warming gravy train for more than a quarter century. Now, with the panic over global warming all but vanished, they have started pushing a new biodiversity crisis. The economic case for global action to stop the destruction of the natural world is even more powerful than the argument for tackling climate change, claims a major report from the United Nations, the Economics of Ecosystems and Biodiversity (TEEB) report. Characteristically, the science behind the biodiversity crisis is even shakier than for global warming.

The words of [the American essayist] Henry Louis Mencken we quoted in *The Resilient Earth* put it best: "The fundamental aim of practical politics is to keep the populace alarmed, and hence clamoring to be led to safety, by menacing it with an endless series of hobgoblins, all of them imaginary." This is a tactic that the UN has turned into an art form. Having succeeded with turning global warming into a "crisis" they are now giving biodiversity a go.

Be safe, enjoy the interglacial [period] and stay skeptical.

EVALUATING THE AUTHOR'S ARGUMENTS:

Doug L. Hoffman's argument hinges on the idea that because we cannot know how many species exist, we cannot say how many are in crisis. How do you think the other authors in this chapter would respond to this line of reasoning? Write one to two sentences for each author. Then, state your opinion: Do you agree with Hoffman? Why or why not?

Viewpoint 5

The IUCN Red List Is the World's Best Measure of Extinction Risk

J.C. Vie, Craig Hilton-Taylor, and Simon N. Stuart

"The IUCN Red List . . . is the world's most comprehensive information source on the global conservation status of plant and animal species."

Each year, the International Union for Conservation of Nature (IUCN) publishes the IUCN Red List, a comprehensive report that tracks biodiversity and monitors species that are facing extinction. In the following viewpoint, J.C. Vie, Craig Hilton-Taylor, and Simon N. Stuart argue that the IUCN Red List is a critical tool for monitoring the world's species and preventing high-risk ones from being lost to extinction. They explain that the IUCN Red List is the most complete global list of threatened species available and that as such, it makes critical assessments of the world's known species and can be used to craft environmental policy and designate habitat protection areas. They conclude that the IUCN Red List is one of the world's best tools for highlighting the problem of biodiversity loss and protecting against it.

J.C. Vie, Craig Hilton-Taylor, and Simon N. Stuart, eds., "The IUCN Red List: A Key Conservation Tool," *Wildlife in a Changing World*, IUCN, 2009, pp. 1–35. http://data.iucn.org/dbtw-wpd/edocs/RL-2009-001.pdf. Reproduced by permission of the International Union for Conservation of Nature.

Vie, Hilton-Taylor, and Stuart work for the International Union for Conservation of Nature.

AS YOU READ, CONSIDER THE FOLLOWING QUESTIONS:
1. According to the authors, for what nine categories does the IUCN Red List provide information regarding whether a species is threatened or not?
2. Approximately what percentage of the world's species do the authors say have been assessed for the IUCN Red List so far?
3. What is the Species Information Service (SIS) as described by the authors?

Biodiversity loss is one of the world's most pressing crises with many species declining to critically low levels and with significant numbers going extinct. At the same time there is growing awareness of how biodiversity supports human livelihoods. Governments and civil society have responded to this challenge by setting clear conservation targets, such as the Convention on Biological Diversity's 2010 target to reduce the current rate of biodiversity loss. In this context, *The IUCN Red List of Threatened Species*™ (hereafter The IUCN Red List) is a clarion call to action in the drive to tackle the extinction crisis, providing essential information on the state of, and trends in, wild species.

A Highly Respected Source of Information

The IUCN Red List Categories and Criteria are widely accepted as the most objective and authoritative system available for assessing the global risk of extinction for species. The IUCN Red List itself is the world's most comprehensive information source on the global conservation status of plant and animal species; . . . it is based on an objective system allowing assignment of any species (except microorganisms) to one of eight Red List Categories based on whether they meet criteria linked to population trend, size and structure and geographic range.

One of The IUCN Red List's main purposes is to highlight those species that are facing a high risk of global extinction. However, it is not just a register of names and associated threat categories. The real power and utility of The IUCN Red List is in what lies beneath: a rich, expert-driven compendium of information on species' ecological requirements, geographic distributions and threats that arms us with the knowledge on what the challenges to nature are, where they are operating, and how to combat them.

The IUCN Red List is not limited to just providing a threat categorization. For an increasing number of species, be they threatened or not, it now provides extensive information covering taxonomy (classification of species), conservation status, geographic distribution, habitat requirements, biology, threats, population, utilization, and conservation actions. Spatial distribution maps are also becoming available for an increasing number of species (almost 20,000 species on The 2008 IUCN Red List have maps). All this information allows scientists to undertake detailed analyses of biodiversity across the globe.

Only about 2.7% of the world's estimated 1.8 million described species have been assessed for The IUCN Red List so far; therefore the number of reported threatened species is much less than the true number at serious risk of extinction. The IUCN Red List is, nevertheless, by far the most complete global list of such species available. . . .

In Barcelona, Spain, at the World Congress of the International Union for Conservation of Nature (IUCN), researchers present their Red List of animal species that are threatened with extinction,

A Sophisticated Information Management System

IUCN has developed the Species Information Service (SIS), an information management tool to collect, manage, process, and report data—to the point of publication on The IUCN Red List. The SIS allows the contributors to participate in the Red List assessment work more easily than was the case in the past. In addition, through improved data exploration capabilities on The IUCN Red List website, SIS is making the world's most accurate, up-to-date information on species, their distribution and conservation status accessible with flexible, easy-to-use tools to support sound environmental decision-making.

The number of species assessed as threatened keeps increasing every year. By 2008, 44,837 species have been assessed; at least 38% of these have been classified as threatened and 804 classified as Extinct. The documented number of threatened species and extinctions is only the tip of the iceberg, as this number depends on the overall number of assessed species; in addition, 5,561 species classified as Data Deficient are possibly threatened. The number of Extinct species is also a very conservative estimate given that for a species to be listed as Extinct requires exhaustive surveys to have been undertaken in all known or likely habitats throughout its historical range, at appropriate times and over a timeframe appropriate to its life cycle and life form. Species that are likely to be Extinct but for which additional surveys might be necessary to eliminate any doubt, are classified in the Critically Endangered Category with a "Possibly Extinct" flag.

More Species Need Assessing

Comprehensive assessments of every known species of mammal, bird, amphibian, shark, reef-building coral, cycad and conifer have been conducted. There are ongoing efforts to complete assessments

> **FAST FACT**
>
> As of October 2010, the IUCN Red List of Threatened Species had evaluated 55,926 species, including mammals, birds, reptiles, amphibians, fishes, eight classes of invertebrates, six classes of plants, and three classes of fungi and protists (microorganisms).

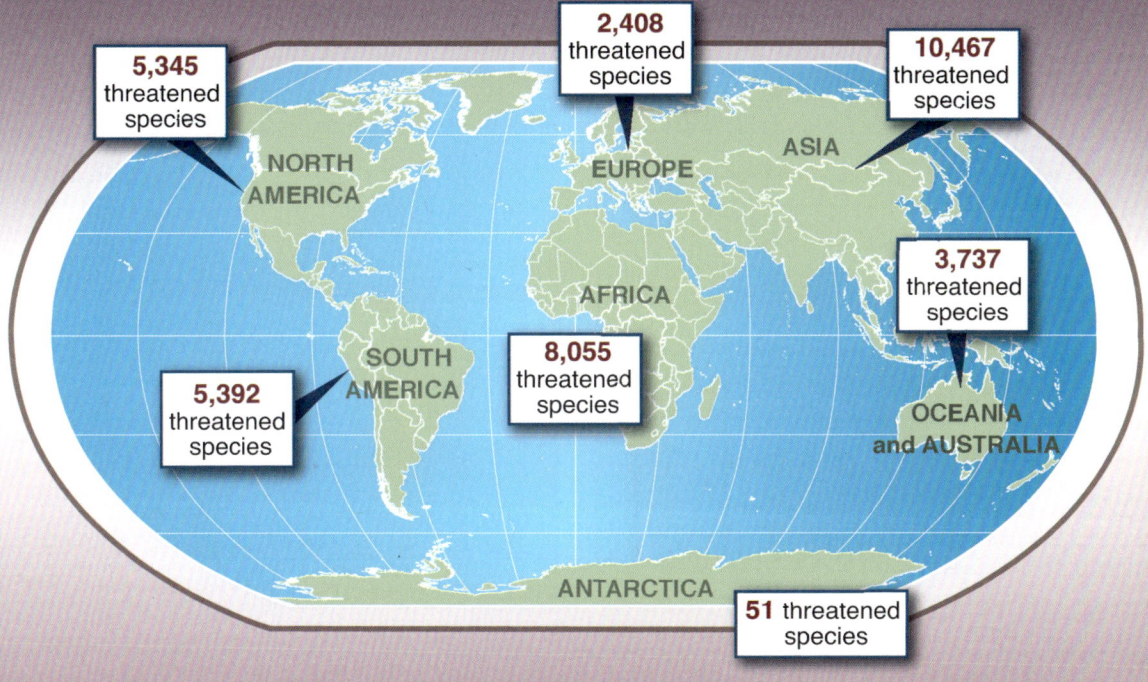

of all reptiles, all fishes, and selected groups of plants and invertebrates.

Around 1.8 million species have been described, yet the estimates of the total number of species on earth range from 2–100 million. We are far from knowing the true status of the earth's biodiversity. Although only a small proportion of the world's species has so far been assessed, this sample indicates how life on earth is faring, how little is known, and how urgent the need is to assess more species.

Despite the limited number of species assessed in relation to the total number of species known, and the significant number of Data

Deficient species included in it, the Red List is still the largest dataset of current information on species. It allows us to measure how little the diversity of life on our planet is known and how urgent the need is to expand the assessment work if we want to be in a position to track progress towards reducing biodiversity loss. . . .

A Multitude of Uses

The IUCN Red List can help answer many important questions, including:

- What is the overall status of biodiversity, and how is it changing over time?
- How does the status of biodiversity vary between regions, countries and sub-national areas?
- What is the rate at which biodiversity is being lost?
- Where is biodiversity being lost most rapidly?
- What are the main drivers of the decline and loss of biodiversity?
- What is the effectiveness and impact of conservation activities? . . .

Red List data (including information on habitat requirements, threats that need to be addressed, and conservation actions that are recommended) can be used to identify species that require specific conservation action, and to help develop the conservation programmes and recovery plans. The data have also been used in the identification of Evolutionary Distinct and Globally Endangered (EDGE) species, unique animals that are often not the focus of significant conservation support.

A Basis for Change

Biological diversity goes beyond species and encompasses ecosystems and genes. However, species remain the well-identified building blocks of biodiversity, and they are easily understood by the public and policy makers alike. By enhancing knowledge on the state of biodiversity, explaining complex species-conservation issues, and highlighting species at risk, The IUCN Red List is attracting increasing attention to the important role that species play if ecosystems are to function properly.

The Red List is increasingly informing academic work (e.g., school home-work assignments, undergraduate essays and dissertations) and many key websites rely on information from The IUCN Red List to help spread their messages and educate the world about conservation issues. Examples include ARKive, Encyclopedia of Life (EOL), Wikipedia, Alliance for Zero Extinction (AZE) and many more. IUCN strives to make The IUCN Red List an important companion to other sites, thus increasing their ability to have conservation impact. The Red List also provides a solid factual basis when drafting funding proposals which seek support for meaningful conservation work.

EVALUATING THE AUTHOR'S ARGUMENTS:

In this viewpoint the authors use facts, statistics, examples, and reasoning to argue that the IUCN Red List is the world's best measure of extinction risk. They do not, however, use any quotations to support their viewpoint. If you were to rewrite this article and insert quotations, what authorities might you quote? Where would you place these quotations and why?

Viewpoint 6

The IUCN Red List Is a Flawed Measure of Extinction Risk

Agence France-Presse (AFP)

> *"The ... (IUCN) 'Red List' of endangered species—likewise a benchmark for policy makers—is now also subject to review."*

In the following viewpoint Agence France-Presse (AFP) correspondents discuss the results of a study that shows that the generally accepted rate of species extinction is exaggerated and needs to be revised. According to the study, scientists have for approximately three decades used a flawed method for estimating extinction rates that puts the extinction rate between two and three times the actual rate. Because the method of estimation used by conservation researchers has been flawed, existing estimates, including those on the IUCN Red List, are subject to review and revision. The study gives hope that humans have more time to prevent the extinction of endangered species, but it also indicates that a lot of research needs to be redone.

AFP, based in Paris, France, is the oldest and one of the largest news agencies in the world, with news centers and correspondents in many countries of the world.

AFP, "Species Loss Far Less Severe than Feared," *The Independent,* May 19, 2011. Copyright © 2011 Independent News & Media PLC. All rights reserved. Reproduced by permission.

AS YOU READ, CONSIDER THE FOLLOWING QUESTIONS:
1. Name two of the coauthors of the study discussed in the viewpoint and the universities where they work.
2. By what amount must the species extinction rate be divided to make the predicted rate of extinction match the actual rate, according to one of the study's coauthors?
3. What is the flawed method of species extinction rate estimation, according to the authors of the study?

The pace at which humans are driving animal and plant species toward extinction through habitat destruction is at least twice as slow as previously thought, according to a study released Wednesday [May 18, 2011].

Earth's biodiversity continues to dwindle due to deforestation, climate change, over-exploitation and chemical runoff into rivers and oceans, said the study, published in *Nature*.

"The evidence is in—humans really are causing extreme extinction rates," said [study] co-author Stephen Hubbell, a professor of ecology and evolutionary biology at the University of California at Los Angeles.

But key measures of species loss in the 2005 UN Millennium Ecosystem Assessment and the 2007 Intergovernmental Panel on Climate Change (IPCC) report are based on "fundamentally flawed" methods that exaggerate the threat of extinction, the researchers said.

The International Union for the Conservation of Nature (IUCN) "Red List" of endangered species—likewise a benchmark for policy makers—is now also subject to review, they said.

FAST FACT

As of January 2010, the IUCN had identified 6,702 species—5,913 of which were animals—as data deficient, a controversial category that means the IUCN lacks enough information to assign a conservation status to them. Critics charge that the category includes many critically endangered species that deserve protection.

Delegates meet at the 2010 Convention on Biological Diversity in Japan to discuss their goal of reducing biodiversity loss. The IUCN Red List of endangered species has stirred many individuals and organizations to action, though many argue the list is flawed.

"Based on a mathematical proof and empirical data, we show that previous estimates should be divided roughly by 2.5," Hubbell told journalists by phone.

"This is welcome news in that we have bought a little time for saving species. But it is unwelcome news because we have to redo a whole lot of research that was done incorrectly."

Up to now, scientists have asserted that species are currently dying out at 100 to 1,000 times the so-called "background rate," the average pace of extinctions over the history of life on Earth.

UN reports have predicted these rates will accelerate tenfold in the coming centuries.

The new study challenges these estimates. "The method has got to be revised. It is not right," said Hubbell.

How did science get it wrong for so long?

Because it is difficult to directly measure extinction rates, scientists used an indirect approach called a "species-area relationship."

This method starts with the number of species found in a given area and then estimates how that number grows as the area expands.

To figure out how many species will remain when the amount of land decreases due to habitat loss, researchers simply reversed the calculations.

But the study, co-authored by Fangliang He of Sun Yat-sen University in Guangzhou [China], shows that the area required to remove the entire population is always larger—usually much larger—than the area needed to make contact with a species for the first time.

"You can't just turn it around to calculate how many species should be left when the area is reduced," said Hubbell.

That, however, is precisely what scientists have done for nearly three decades, giving rise to a glaring discrepancy between what models predicted and what was observed on the ground or in the sea.

Dire forecasts in the early 1980s said that as many as half of species on Earth would disappear by 2000. "Obviously that didn't happen," Hubbell said.

But rather than question the methods, scientists developed a concept called "extinction debt" to explain the gap.

Species in decline, according to this logic, are doomed to disappear even if it takes decades or longer for the last individuals to die out.

But extinction debt, it turns out, almost certainly does not exist.

"It is kind of shocking" that no one spotted the error earlier, said Hubbell. "What this shows is that many scientists can be led away from the right answer by thinking about the problem in the wrong way."

Human encroachment is the main driver of species extinction. Only 20 percent of forests are still in a wild state, and nearly 40 percent of the planet's ice-free land is now given over to agriculture.

Some three-quarters of all species are thought to live in rain forests, which are disappearing at the rate of about half-a-percent per year.

EVALUATING THE AUTHOR'S ARGUMENTS:

The authors of the study discussed in this viewpoint argue that species are becoming extinct at approximately half the predicted rate. Does this information affect how serious a problem you think species extinction should be considered? Discuss your answer using evidence from this and the previous viewpoint.

Chapter 2

What Are the Most Significant Threats to Endangered Species?

The Deepwater Horizon *oil platform explosion and the subsequent massive oil spill revived debate about which human activities constitute threats to animal and marine life.*

Viewpoint 1

Climate Change Is a Significant Threat to Plant and Animal Species

International Council for Local Environmental Initiatives (ICLEI)

"Current rates of climate change have already resulted in species composition changes."

ICLEI is one of a network of partners in Countdown 2010 that work together to tackle the causes of biodiversity loss. The Countdown 2010 sponsors include the International Union for Conservation of Nature, the Royal Society for the Protection of Birds, and government ministries from Austria, Belgium, Denmark, Switzerland, Italy, Ireland, and many others. In the following viewpoint the author argues that a main culprit of biodiversity loss is climate change. A warming climate will have disastrous effects on species' habitats and reproductive cycles, the author warns. An increase in severe weather further threatens species' habitats, mating behaviors, and ability to find food. The author calls on local and regional authorities to take actions that preserve habitat, prevent climate change, and protect species.

ICLEI—Local Governments for Sustainability, "Biodiversity and Climate Change," Countdown 2010, 2008. Reproduced by permission.

AS YOU READ, CONSIDER THE FOLLOWING QUESTIONS:
1. What does Countdown 2010 warn will push many species toward the poles? What problem does the author say this shift will cause?
2. According to the author, what kind of impact does climate change have on urban areas? List at least three impacts.
3. What process "sequesters" carbon dioxide from the atmosphere, as explained in the viewpoint?

Over the course of history, ecosystems have always had to adapt to changing climatic conditions. The current rate of climate change, however, is higher than ever recorded. It is now obvious that humans have impacted biodiversity loss—directly through the destruction of habitats, and indirectly through climate change.

The Effect of Climate Change on Species

Current rates of climate change have already resulted in species composition changes. As the climate warms up or cools down, many local species have to shift from their current habitat to areas better suited to their needs. This means that with rising average temperatures many species will experience a range shift towards the poles, potentially pushing out existing species in those areas. In other cases warming will cause species to shift their ranges upwards along altitudinal gradients, with the same effect.

Changing temperatures will also influence their reproductive cycles, their growth patterns and, also as a result of range shifts, the interaction between species. All this may occur over time frames as short as decades.

The Effect on Cities

Affected species are likely to include those to which humankind has attached various values (e.g. cultural emblems, indigenous crops, plants that typically mark the landscape). This will also include wild plants that are locally used, such as medicinal herbs, mushrooms and wild flowers. Examples of the urban impacts of such species changes are:

- Loss of trees in streets, gardens and parks, as changing temperatures add stress and reduce their resilience to pests;
- Loss of species and damage of (municipal) forests, reducing economic gains as well as recreational values;
- Risk of collapsing waste water treatment systems as micro-organisms are vulnerable to temperature differences;
- Damages to flora and fauna through the immigrating of (alien) species;
- Risks to human health through the immigration of disease carrying insects such as mosquitoes.

"Global Warming2," cartoon by Deng Coy Miel and PoliticalCartoons.com, April 1, 2007. Copyright © 2007 Deng Coy Miel, Singapore, and PoliticalCartoons.com. All rights reserved.

Changes to local biological diversity and species composition poses tremendous challenges to conservation planning and implementation. Common conservation practices need to be revised in order to accommodate the current and future challenges resulting from climate change.

If rapid and irreversible change in biodiversity is to be avoided, conservation strategies need to focus more on supporting the species' natural capacity to adapt to change. Beyond a moral obligation to act, helping species to adapt may also avoid the loss of important ecosystem services and the cultural and economic values attached to particular species. . . .

Protect Species, Fight Climate Change

Biodiversity also plays a crucial but often underestimated role in the mitigation of climate change. Mitigation refers to actions that reduce the extent of global warming. The biological diversity of ecosystems is a key factor in ensuring the natural processes undertaken by ecosystems.

One of these processes is growth. As they grow, plants, fungi and soil bacteria work together to bind carbon dioxide [CO_2] gas from the atmosphere into the soil, wood and other organic matter. This process 'sequesters' carbon dioxide from the atmosphere, thereby helping to reduce the amount of this greenhouse gas, which is most responsible for global warming.

The release of CO_2 through deforestation and land use change accounts for as much as 25% of total human-induced greenhouse gas emissions. Maintaining local biodiversity and increasing urban green space, in particular forest areas, therefore are significant and effective contributions towards protecting the global climate.

Apart from conserving green areas, local and regional authorities can provide the regulatory framework for encouraging vegetation growth on private properties.

Increasing the green areas in densely populated areas does not only contribute to global climate protection. Trees and other vegetation also help improve the local air quality, provide shade and lead to a cooler and more humid microclimate, which is particularly relevant in hot climates and seasons. Investing in global climate protection will quickly pay off locally and improve the quality of life in cities and towns.

Rain forest land in Brazil is cleared for crop use. Deforestation and land use changes, both caused by humans, make up nearly 25 percent of total greenhouse gas emissions.

A Changing Climate Brings Severe Weather

As the climate changes, extreme weather events such as storms, floods, droughts and heat waves are expected to become more intense and unpredictable.

Healthy ecosystems play a crucial role in mitigating the impact of climate-induced disasters. For example, a biologically diverse and healthy forest ecosystem has a high capacity to absorb torrential rain. It provides tree cover and undergrowth that can reduce the erosive impact of intense precipitation, slow down the surface run-off and support the seepage of rain water into the soil and lower rock beds. These processes help reduce the risk of flash floods, mud slides and soil erosion. Conserving a patch of native vegetation may therefore be a key component of integrated disaster risk reduction in the face of climate change.

Local and regional authorities will be called upon to take action to effectively use their regulatory capacity to help infrastructure systems and people adapt to a changing climate. The destructive impact of climate-related disasters on human settlements depends considerably on the ability of local and regional authorities to effectively factor climate change risks in infrastructure planning and the design of municipal services.

Biodiversity management therefore needs to become integrated with disaster risk reduction planning and emergency response. For example, local and regional authorities can help reduce flood risks by protecting and restoring riverine and coastal vegetation. This will help regulate a more even flow of water in a catchment, reducing the impacts of extreme precipitation, storm surges or coastal wave action. In vegetated areas, the rate of water seepage into the ground is also higher, which reduces the impacts of droughts.

All these measures will support local economic and infrastructure systems to adapt to a changing climate. If carefully planned [and] based on local indicators for climate change, even technologically simple and inexpensive measures can result in tremendous benefits. While national governments in many countries provide national adaptation plans, local and regional authorities have the challenging task to gather local data on climate change and making responsible decisions for local adaptation to climate change.

Such comprehensive 'anticipatory adaptation' will need to focus on technological, socio-economic and ecological support mechanisms alike. Conserving healthy ecosystems and promoting the adaptive capacity of species helps ensure that urban and rural environments can retain their 'fitness' and continue to provide the ecosystem services so vital for their inhabitants, despite the uncertainties of a changing local climate.

> **FAST FACT**
>
> In 2010 climate-change researchers from the National Snow and Ice Data Center in Colorado released study results predicting that Arctic summer sea ice will disappear by 2050. This would cause the world's 20,000–25,000 polar bears to vanish from two-thirds of their range by midcentury and be nearly extinct by 2100.

Cities Can and Must Take Action

Local and regional authorities are key players in coordinating and implementing biodiversity management measures that take climate change into account.

For helping species to adapt to climate change, they can:

- Adapt zoning and urban development plans to increase the connectivity of habitats to enable species to migrate more easily;
- Protect biologically diverse habitats and plan for an expansion of protected areas to increase the probability for species' local survival despite climate change;

For protecting the climate and to mitigate further climate change, local and regional authorities can:

- Participate in climate protection programs (such as the Cities for Climate Protection Campaign) that effectively reduce greenhouse gas emissions; for example through an extension of public transport, energy efficiency measures and the tapping of renewable energy sources;
- Invest in the planting of trees to increase carbon sequestration;
- Provide incentives for private and corporate stakeholders to invest in renewable energy and energy efficiency.

Lastly, as climate change can no longer be avoided, local and regional authorities need to regulate and plan for the adaptation of human activity to a changing climate.

This can include:

- Increasing tree cover and green space in urban areas to cool local temperatures down during the hot season and create more livable microclimates;
- Protect and restore riverine or coastal vegetation for reducing the risks of flooding as a result of extreme weather events;
- Rehabilitate and diversify municipal forests and wetlands to help regulate a more evenly distributed flow in watersheds.

These are only a few examples of local and regional action for integrated biodiversity management that should help inspire creative planning and management processes suited for tackling the local and regional specific impacts of climate change.

EVALUATING THE AUTHOR'S ARGUMENTS:

In this viewpoint the author uses facts, statistics, examples, and reasoning to make the argument that climate change threatens the well-being of plant and animal species. The author does not, however, use any quotations to support that point. If you were to rewrite this article and insert quotations, what authorities might you quote? Where would you place the quotations, and why?

Viewpoint 2

Plant and Animal Species Can Adapt to Climate Change

Josef Reichholf, interviewed by *Spiegel*

"The warmer a region is, the more diverse are its species."

In the following viewpoint biologist Josef Reichholf is interviewed by the German newsmagazine *Spiegel* and argues that a warmer climate does not threaten plant or animal species. Reichholf suggests that species are very good at adapting to warmer temperatures—this is why bears, birds, and other creatures typically live in multiple types of climates. In his opinion, climate change does not pose nearly as much of a threat to species as does human development and hunting. Reichholf concludes that a warmer climate will yield more food, better habitat, and more survivable ecological conditions, all of which will help plants and animals thrive.

Reichholf is a professor of zoology at the State Zoological Collection in Munich, Germany.

Josef Reichholf, "We Are Children of the Tropics," *Spiegel Online*, May 8, 2007. www.spiegel.de. Copyright © 2007 by *Spiegel Online*. Reproduced by permission of the publisher and the author.

AS YOU READ, CONSIDER THE FOLLOWING QUESTIONS:
1. In what era does Reichholf say biodiversity reached its peak? What were temperatures like then?
2. How does the wren factor into Reichholf's argument about how climate change affects species?
3. What does Reichholf say is a greater threat to polar bears than climate change?

SPIEGEL: *Mr. Reichholf, are you worried about global warming?*
     Josef Reichholf: No. Personally, I'm even looking forward to a milder climate. But it will also not pose any major problems for mankind as a whole.
  Where does your optimism come from?
  The vast majority of people today already live under warmer and, in many cases, far more extreme conditions than we pampered Central Europeans. Homo sapiens is the only biological species that can handle practically any type of climate on earth—from the deserts to the polar regions, from the constantly humid tropics to the high altitudes of the Andes. Not even the animals that follow human society most closely, the rats, have developed such an astonishing ability to adapt in the course of evolution.
  In what sort of climate does man feel most comfortable?
  Biologically speaking, we are children of the tropics. Wherever man lives, he artificially creates tropical living conditions. We do this with warm clothing, and with heated offices and homes. A tropical temperature of about 27 degrees Celsius (80 degrees Fahrenheit) constantly prevails underneath our clothing.

Climate Change Does Not Threaten Animals and Plants
But, as an ecologist, aren't you at least concerned about animals and plants?
  Many species are certainly threatened, but not by climate change. The true danger comes from the destruction of habitats, such as the rampant deforestation of species-rich tropical forests. Particularly as a conservationist, I believe that focusing on the greenhouse effect is very dangerous. The climate is increasingly being turned into a

Is Global Warming Good for Plants?

Most plants thrive in a CO_2-rich environment. The following chart shows various plants that grow up to 124 percent larger in air that has been enriched with CO_2. As a result, some argue, a warmer world will be good for plant and crop yields.

Growth Response to 300 ppm* Additional CO_2

	Mean % Increase
Grains	
Barley	41.5%
Rice	34.3%
Wheat	33.0%
Vegetables	
Green Beans	64.3%
Soybeans	47.6%
White Potatoes	29.5%
Sweet Potatoes	33.7%
Corn	21.3%
Carrots	77.8%
Fruits	
Cantaloupe	4.7%
Sweet Cherries	59.8%
Strawberries	42.8%
Tomatoes	31.9%
Trees	
Black Cottonwood	124.0%
Red Maple	44.2%
Northern Red Oak	53.3%
Loblolly Pine	61.9%

*ppm = parts per million.

Taken from: Center for the Study of Carbon Dioxide and Global Change, 2011; PlantsNeedCO2.com.

scapegoat, to deflect attention from other environmental crimes. A typical example is the misleading debate over catastrophic flooding, which is in fact caused by too much development along rivers and not by more extreme weather events, which we can't change anyway.

What do you see as the greatest threat to plants and animals?

Industrial agriculture is the number one killer of species in Germany. With their monocultures and over-fertilized fields, farmers have radically impaired the living conditions for many animals and plants. Many species have already fled from the countryside to the cities, which have been transformed into havens of biodiversity. We are also seeing another interesting phenomenon: Major cities, like Hamburg, Berlin and Munich, have formed heat islands where the climate has been two or three degrees warmer than in the surrounding countryside for decades. If higher temperatures are truly so bad, why do more and more animals and plants feel so comfortable in our cities?

> **FAST FACT**
>
> Population biologist Camille Parmesan reported in a March 2011 *Nature* interview that, consistent with a warming world, spring now begins two weeks earlier. This means that almost two-thirds of species, including birds, frogs, butterflies, and trees, are breeding or blooming earlier and that more than 50 percent are changing where they live.

Climate Change Will Help Species Thrive

And what is your view of the prognoses that global warming will cause up to 30 percent of all animal species to become extinct?

It's nothing but fear-mongering, for which there is no concrete evidence. On the contrary, there is much to be said for the argument that warming temperatures promote biodiversity. There is a clear relationship between biodiversity and temperature. The number of species increases exponentially from the regions near the poles across the moderate latitudes and to the equator. To put it succinctly, the warmer a region is, the more diverse are its species.

Are you saying that the greenhouse effect could even help improve biodiversity in the long term?

Exactly. And this can also be clearly inferred from the insights of evolutionary biology. Biodiversity reached its peak at the end of the tertiary age, a few million years ago, when it was much warmer than it is today. The development went in a completely different direction when the ice ages came and temperatures dropped, causing a massive extinction of species, especially in the north. This also explains why Europe has such a high capacity to absorb species from warmer regions. It just so happens that we have many unoccupied ecological niches in our less biodiverse part of the world.

In other words, for you global warming means more flourishing landscapes on the planet?

Indeed. When it becomes warmer, many species receive new habitats. The overall picture is clearly positive, as long as we don't destroy the newly developing habitats right away by intervening in nature in other ways. It's no accident that most of the species on Germany's red list of endangered species are the heat-loving species. Many of them could be given new opportunities to survive in Germany.

Species Will Adapt to Warmer Temperatures

But aren't you underestimating the rapid pace of the current warming? Many animals and plants are unable to adapt quickly enough to a changing climate.

This claim is already contradicted by the fact that there have been much faster climate fluctuations in the past, which did not automatically lead to a global extinction of species. As a biologist, I can tell you that only the fewest animals and plants are accustomed to rigid climate conditions. Take our little wren, for example. Many would call it a sensitive little songbird. But the wren thrives just as well in Stockholm [Sweden] as it does in Munich or Rome. It even lives above the tree line in the Alps. The only places we don't see wrens are where there are no bushes or trees growing at all.

But there are certainly animals that live in very limited niches. For example, how would polar bears survive global warming?

Then let me ask you in return: How did the polar bear survive the last warm period? Perhaps [the polar bear named] Knut at the Berlin Zoo is an exception, but polar bears in the wild don't exactly survive by sucking on ice. Seals are the polar bear's most important source of food, and the Canadians slaughter tens of thousands of them every

The author points to the common wren as an example of species adaptation. The wren can live wherever there are trees—and sometimes even above the tree line.

spring. That's why life is becoming more and more difficult for polar bears, and not because it's getting warmer. Look at the polar bear's close relative, the brown bear. It is found across a broad geographic region, ranging from Europe across the Near East and North Asia, to Canada and the United States. Whether bears survive will depend on human beings, not the climate.

Is there really no plant or animal species that isn't at risk of extinction because of a further rise in temperatures?

I certainly can't think of any. There are a few flatworms that can only exist in icy cold springs. These creatures do in fact appear to be disappearing in places where the springs are warming up. But this could also be a coincidence, because the closest relatives of these worms tolerate a much broader temperature spectrum.

Do Not Fear Warmer Times

Conversely, should we be worried that malaria, as a result of global warming, will break out in our latitude once again?

That's another one of those myths. Many people truly believe that malaria will spread as temperatures rise. But malaria isn't even a true tropical disease. In the 19th century, thousands of people in Europe, including Germany, the Netherlands and even Scandinavia, died of malaria, even though they had never gone abroad. That's because this disease was still prevalent in northern and central Europe in previous centuries. We only managed to eliminate malaria in Europe by quarantining the sick, improving hygiene and draining swamps. That's why I consider it virtually impossible that malaria would return to us purely because of climate change. If it does appear, it'll be because it has been brought in somewhere.

Why has it become a dogma that we should be afraid of warmer times?

It's a mystery to me. As recently as the 1960s, people were more concerned about a new ice age—and that would indeed pose a great danger to us. The most catastrophic eras were those in which the weather became worse, not phases of warmer climates. Precisely because we have to feed a growing population on this planet, we should in fact embrace a warmer climate. In warmer regions it takes far less effort to ensure survival.

> ### EVALUATING THE AUTHOR'S ARGUMENTS:
>
> Josef Reichholf and Countdown 2010, the author of the previous viewpoint, agree that loss of habitat threatens plant and animal species. Yet they disagree on what causes habitat loss. Countdown 2010 says it is due to climate change; Reichholf says it is due to human development. In your opinion, which author made the better argument? Why? List at least one piece of evidence that swayed you.

Viewpoint 3

Offshore Oil Drilling Endangers Wildlife

Julia Whitty

> "In the wake of the BP [oil] spill, there's been a spike in sea turtle deaths."

Offshore drilling is catastrophic for marine species argues Julia Whitty in the following viewpoint. She discusses the 2010 oil spill caused by an explosion on a British Petroleum oil rig, the *Deepwater Horizon*, in the Gulf of Mexico. Labeled as one of the worst human-made disasters in American history, the oil spill jeopardized the health and lives of numerous species living in the gulf. Dolphins, birds, turtles, whales, and manatees are just a few of the creatures at risk. In addition to outright killing of animals, Whitty contends that the spill poisoned survivors' food supplies, polluted their bodies, and tainted the habitat they rely on to lay eggs and mate. She concludes that deepwater drilling is incredibly risky for marine life and that the full ecological consequences of the 2010 spill will not be known for years.

Whitty is a former documentary filmmaker specializing in science and the natu-

Julia Whitty, "The BP Cover-Up," *Mother Jones,* September/October 2010. Copyright © 2010 Foundation for National Progress. Reproduced by permission.

ral world. She blogs about environmental issues at *Deep Blue Home* (http://deepbluehome.blogspot.com).

AS YOU READ, CONSIDER THE FOLLOWING QUESTIONS:
1. What are the three consequences that Whitty says oily water has on dolphins?
2. Name at least three ways the author says oil spills affect birds.
3. According to Whitty, how many sperm whale deaths could endanger the entire sperm whale population?

Six weeks after the Deepwater Horizon explosion [in spring 2010], I'm aboard a small inflatable Greenpeace boat, bucking the marshy waters of Barataria Bay, Louisiana. A tide change is under way. Incoming and outgoing waters are flowing in opposing directions, battling each other in current lines inked with oil. A continuous flow of vessels chug through the pass—tugboats, barges, mud boats, seiners, trawlers, pirogues, airboats, sportfishers, pleasure cruisers. Some carry crews to and from the thousands of other drilling platforms puncturing the seafloor of the Gulf of Mexico, but the majority are now laden with containment boom and BP [British Petroleum] cleanup crews.

Dolphins are swimming in the pass too, a few dozen of an estimated 138 to 238 bottlenose dolphins that call Barataria Bay home. They're hugging the greasy waves of the tidal rip. Like bottlenose dolphins the world over, and like much marine life in general, they're exploiting the edge where waters of different provenance (temperature, salinity, velocity) hide predators from prey and vice versa. Along these edges, the sensory systems of the sea—sight, sound, pressure wave, magnetic field—are dimmed or distorted, making it difficult to see from one side through to the other. Bottlenose dolphins use the distortions as natural hunting blinds.

Oil Is Toxic to Life

These waters have been off-limits to human fishers for weeks. But nobody told the dolphins. They're actively fishing the tidal rip and

Shown here is an aerial view of oil-saturated Barataria Bay in Louisiana. The bay is home to many species of wildlife, including dolphins.

following trawlers' dragging boom, because these are the same boats that sometimes give them food in the form of bycatch [undesirable fish] thrown overboard.

As best we know, the dolphins of Barataria Bay comprise a closed population whose members rarely if ever leave the bay. In theory, they could now exit, but in all likelihood they're trapped here by multiple barriers: by oily waters, by seasonal tradition, by cultural habit, by territorial boundaries, and by the availability of food—including fish and other marine life that may be trying to escape the oil by swimming inshore. At the moment, the dolphins are feeding as best they can in home waters that will likely kill them.

Rick Steiner, a conservation-specialist from the University of Alaska who's studied the effects of the *Exxon Valdez* spill [off the coast of Alaska in 1989] for the past 21 years, discusses these possibilities as we look on helplessly. "The dolphins aspirate oily fumes through their blowholes," he says. "They're eating fish exposed to oil. They're getting oil in all their orifices [body openings]. They're bathed in a continual soup of oil. There's nowhere to go to get away from it. We know from the *Exxon Valdez* that even those animals not killed outright suffer lesions in their organs including the brain. They go blind. They experience reproductive failures, changes in their blood chemistry, and possibly multigenerational changes passed down to offspring never even exposed to the oil."

A few hundred yards away, tucked into the marsh grass on Grand Isle State Park, we see a dead dolphin, half-skeletonized, half-mummified. In the heat and humidity of coastal Louisiana, it is hard to tell if it'd been dead a week or a month. We do know that dead dolphins are washing up along the Gulf Coast in higher-than-normal numbers. We don't know how many more have died at sea and sunk, never to be counted. On the beach surrounding the dead dolphin are hundreds of hermit crabs coated with a chocolatey syrup of oil, their tracks up the beach splattered as they fled the foul waters. The oil washing ashore is still actively bubbling. "Even though this concoction may have exploded from the well a month ago and has been wending its way ashore ever since, it's still full of volatile compounds like benzene," says Steiner. "Benzene's a known carcinogen, dangerous to human life, too."

> **FAST FACT**
>
> The US Fish & Wildlife Service reported, as of January 25, 2011, that it had collected 6,124 birds, 608 sea turtles, and 100 mammals (including dolphins) killed by the 2010 *Deepwater Horizon* oil spill in the Gulf of Mexico. Another 2,537 visibly oiled animals were collected alive; about 1,650 of these were eventually released back into the wild.

An Oily Hospice

Barataria Bay has become a hospice wilderness, full of dying plants and animals. Nearly all the marshy islands are oiled. The oyster beds covering 10 percent of the bay are dead or dying and now closed to human harvesting. The post-larval brown shrimp migrating into the bay (the estuaries of Louisiana and Texas are home to the highest densities of brown shrimp in US waters) are running an oily gauntlet. So are the speckled trout that normally feast on brown shrimp during their own breeding season. For the first time in my bird-watching life, I've seen multitudes of clapper rails—notoriously secretive marsh-dwelling birds—running down levees and roads in broad daylight trying to escape the oiled wetlands.

The fate of the marshes is inextricably linked to the fate of the deep ocean—and vice versa. The deep ocean seeds the marshes with the larvae of fish and invertebrates, which then repopulate the deep in their juvenile or adult stages....

At Queen Bess Island, an important seabird rookery near the mouth of Barataria Bay, Steiner and I watch oily brown pelicans trying to preen themselves clean. I visited this same island a week ago; the downy pelican chicks who were still in the nest then are today slipping on oily rocks at the waterline. Where last week there were still a few dozen white pelicans, now there are only two, standing uncharacteristically alone, wings drooping in stress. Steiner points out the pelicans flying overhead, their bellies coated with oil. "Even those birds who are managing to avoid diving into contaminated water to feed are inadvertently floating on it," he says.

Death by Oil

Death by oil is a horrible way to go. Necropsies on birds reveal hypothermia resulting from oiled feathers, malnutrition resulting from the hypothermia, anemia from the shock and stress of hunger, and poisoning from the oil ingested and inhaled during preening. Although a few birds will escape the immediate lethal effects their eggs and chicks will not....

As bad as it is in Barataria Bay, it's only the beginning....

[Director of the Louisiana Universities Marine Consortium Nancy] Rabalais is worried about the species already under enormous stress from a host of other environmental problems in the Gulf: dead zones, overfishing, chronic oil pollution, seismic testing for oil and natural gas, coastal erosion. "Brown pelicans just came off the endangered species list," she says, "and now some of their most important breeding rookeries are getting hit with oil." She's concerned about critically

The Creatures of the Gulf

The average depth of the Gulf of Mexico is just over 5,000 feet. This is the zone in which the *Deepwater Horizon* explosion spilled millions of gallons of oil and also where several different types of animals live.

Taken from: Julia Whitty, "The BP Cover-Up," *Mother Jones*, September/October 2010.

endangered Kemp's Ridley sea turtles, the rarest on Earth, a species that faced mortal threat from the 140 million-gallon spill at [Mexico's] Ixtoc I drilling platform in the Gulf in 1979. Kemp's Ridleys breed almost exclusively in the Gulf, with virtually every female returning to lay her eggs on a stretch of beach south of the Texas border.

Sea Turtles, Whales, and Other Species at Risk

In the wake of the BP spill, there's been a spike in sea turtle deaths, the majority of them Kemp's Ridleys. The number is certain to rise, since some sea turtles feed in the DSL [deep scattering layer of ocean organisms], and most enjoy a meal of jellyfish. Sadly, they also eat blobs of oil they mistake for jellyfish. According to some reports, sea turtles have been roasted alive in the surface-oil patches burning offshore. Hundreds more have drowned since the disaster began. . . .

Rabalais and others also worry about the Gulf's sperm whales, which feed on squid living in the deep scattering layer. An estimated 1,665 sperm whales inhabit (and perhaps never leave) the northern waters of the Gulf. A recent National Oceanic and Atmospheric Administration (NOAA) assessment calculated that even three additional deaths (by other than natural causes) could endanger the entire sperm whale population, since the whales breed infrequently and only in midlife. The whales favor the deep waters of Mississippi Canyon—the location of the Deepwater Horizon wellhead. On numerous occasions, they've been seen swimming through thick oil in that region. And it's not only sperm whales. The Gulf is home to 29 species of cetaceans, many of which feed on the DSL, including spinner dolphins, spotted dolphins, pilot whales, killer whales, and many secretive deep divers such as beaked and bottlenose whales. The filter-feeding whales—including the Gulf's tiny isolated population of Bryde's whales, plus humpbacks, fins, minkes, and sei, many of which are DSL feeders—are vulnerable a whole different way, since oil fouls their baleen (sievelike teeth), dooming them to starvation.

And then there are the 400 Florida manatees, a species classified as vulnerable to extinction, that migrate to Louisiana waters each summer. This year they'll be feeding in oily water on oiled algae and cordgrass.

EVALUATING THE AUTHOR'S ARGUMENTS:

To make her argument Julia Whitty catalogues the ways in which numerous marine species were affected by the 2010 oil spill in the Gulf of Mexico. What might Ronald Bailey, author of the following viewpoint, have to say about her approach? After reading both viewpoints, with which author do you agree regarding the extent to which offshore drilling endangers wildlife? List at least two pieces of evidence that swayed you.

Viewpoint 4

The Benefits of Offshore Oil Drilling Outweigh the Risks to Wildlife

Ronald Bailey

"The benefits of producing offshore oil greatly outweigh the costs."

Ronald Bailey is the science correspondent for *Reason* magazine, a publication espousing libertarian political principles. Although Bailey agrees it is sad that wildlife are threatened when oil spills occur, he argues that in the grand scheme of things, the production of offshore oil brings in enough revenue to make such environmental accidents worth it. He explores several scenarios in which the revenue generated from offshore oil drilling far exceeds the costs of cleaning up environmental damage incurred from the process of production. Bailey says calm heads must prevail when discussing offshore oil drilling. He encourages Americans not to get caught up in dramatic pictures of oil-stained wildlife. Instead, he urges readers to remember that

Ronald Bailey, "Weighing the Benefits & Costs of Offshore Drilling," *Reason*, May 4, 2010. Reproduced by permission of *Reason* magazine and Reason.com.

offshore drilling is an important revenue-generator and its benefits greatly outweigh its costs.

AS YOU READ, CONSIDER THE FOLLOWING QUESTIONS:
1. What does the word *trade-off* mean in the context of the viewpoint?
2. How many billions of dollars would be generated in revenue if 10 billion barrels of oil were produced at fifty dollars per barrel, according to Bailey?
3. What, according to Bailey, is a trial-and-error process?

Two weeks ago [in April 2010] BP's [British Petroleum's] *Deepwater Horizon* oil drilling rig in the Gulf of Mexico exploded, killing 11 workers. The exploratory well began gushing oil at an estimated rate of 5,000 barrels per day when the blowout prevention system failed. The growing oil slick menaces the marshes and beaches of Louisiana, Mississippi, Alabama, and Florida. Should the slick come ashore, previous research suggests the deleterious effects on fisheries and wildlife would be substantial and long-lasting.

As someone who has enjoyed the sugar white sands of Alabama's beaches, it is a terrible shame that they are at risk of being despoiled by oily muck. But as someone who also enjoys the conveniences of modern civilization including the on-demand mobility offered by airplanes and automobiles that enable me to visit those beaches, I understand trade-offs.

Use Reason, Not "Pictures of Oily Birds"

Opponents of offshore drilling have jumped on the spill as evidence that offshore drilling is inherently dangerous, and not worth the risk. They see the blowout as evidence that the recently lifted moratorium on offshore drilling in parts of the outer continental shelf should be reinstated. Miyoko Sakashita of the Center for Biological Diversity decried "the absurdity of the claims by the oil industry and politicians beholden to that industry that offshore oil and gas development is safe." As a consequence, the center is urging the [Barack] Obama administration "to reinstitute a moratorium on new offshore oil leasing, exploration, and development on all our coasts." The Natural Resources Defense Council is also calling for a "time-out" on any further offshore oil drilling until an independent investigation of the BP spill is completed. On April 30, [2010,] the Obama administration heeded the call for a time-out and halted plans to expand offshore drilling until an investigation into the causes of the BP blowout are complete.

But in deciding whether or not to continue offshore exploration for oil and gas, a calm quantitative approach makes more sense than a rush to ban drilling after seeing some pictures of oily birds. It would be useful to figure out if the costs, economic and ecological, outweigh the benefits of producing offshore oil and gas. Luckily, a recent study by Georgetown University economist Robert Hahn and Milken Institute economist Peter Passell offers some insight to this question. Published in the December 2009 issue of *Energy Economics*, their study, "The economics of allowing more U.S. oil drilling," finds that the benefits of producing offshore oil greatly outweigh the costs.

> **Fast Fact**
> A March 2011 Gallup Poll found that 60 percent of adult Americans favor increasing offshore drilling for oil and gas in US coastal areas. The poll also showed that 49 percent of Americans favor opening Alaska's Arctic National Wildlife Refuge for oil exploration, the highest level of support since Gallup first asked the question in 2002.

Oil Pays More than It Costs

In their analysis, Hahn and Passell look at three types of benefits: producer revenues, lower prices to consumers, and less fluctuation in oil prices. These benefits are considered in a scenario in which oil is priced at $50 per barrel, and in another in which it goes for $100 per barrel. (The [April 2010] price is around $85 per barrel.) At $50 per barrel they estimate that 10 billion barrels of oil would be recoverable from the off-limits outer continental shelf, and at $100 this rises to 11.5 billion barrels.

On the cost side of the ledger they calculate that it would cost $17 per barrel to produce offshore oil at $50 per barrel and $20 per barrel at $100 per barrel. They incorporate a Minerals Management Service estimate of $700 million as the cost of the environmental damage caused by producing 10 billion barrels of oil offshore. They include an estimate of damage caused by greenhouse gases produced by burning the oil as fuel, and the direct costs of local air pollution, and traffic congestion and accidents. So what did they find?

At $50 per barrel, the benefits of offshore oil production in the formerly off-limits areas of the outer continental shelf would garner

Proponents of offshore oil drilling say benefits include increased revenues for oil producers, lower prices for consumers, and stabilization of oil prices.

$492 billion in revenues, $42 billion in lower oil prices, and reduce the cost of oil price disruptions by $42 billion, yielding total benefits of $578 billion. The direct drilling costs would come to $166 billion, environmental costs $1 billion, greenhouse gas damages $1 billion, local air pollution $28 billion, traffic congestion $28 billion, and traffic accidents $32 billion, for a total cost amounting to $255 billion. So at $50 per barrel the benefits of producing 10 billion barrels of offshore oil would be $323 billion greater than its costs.

At $100 per barrel, outer continental shelf oil production of 11.5 billion barrels of oil would reap $1.15 trillion in revenues, lower oil prices by $99 billion, and reduce the costs of price disruptions by $51 billion, resulting in total benefits of $1.3 trillion. Drilling costs would be $238 billion, environmental costs and greenhouse gas damages would total $2 billion, the costs of local air pollution, traffic congestion, and traffic accidents would be $22 billion, $33 billion, and $38 billion respectively. So the total costs of producing 11.5 billion barrels of offshore oil would be $332 billion. Hahn and Passell calculate that at $100 per barrel, the net benefits of producing offshore oil would come to $967 billion, or a trillion dollars. They note that even if the total costs were doubled in both scenarios, "the qualitative conclusion that resource development passes any plausible benefit-cost test still holds."

Wildlife and Habitat Can Be Cleaned Up

But perhaps the environmental costs used by Hahn and Passell are too low. Could they be wrong about the cost of greenhouse emissions? Hahn and Passell note that even at the highest social cost of carbon at $321 per ton suggested by British economist Nicholas Stern, the total benefits of producing offshore oil are still positive. In that case, the net benefits drop from $325 billion to $120 billion at $50 per barrel, and from $975 billion to $725 billion at $100 per barrel.

As for other environmental impacts, analysts at the Environmental Protection Agency (EPA) have devised a Basic Oil Spill Cost Estimation Model to try to figure out the costs of various types of spills. For example, the EPA model projects that the socioeconomic costs of spills over a million gallons is about $60 per gallon and the environmental costs are $30 per gallon. So if the BP blowout continues as-is for a total of 50 days, it will spew 10 million gallons into the Gulf, resulting in $900 million in costs. Applying the model's highest

Oil and Gas Drilling Does Not Significantly Pollute the Marine Environment

The National Research Council of the National Academies found that oil and gas drilling accounts for only about 1 percent of all petroleum discharges into marine environments in North America. Land-based river runoff and recreational vehicles such as jet skis and boats are more significant sources of petroleum pollution.

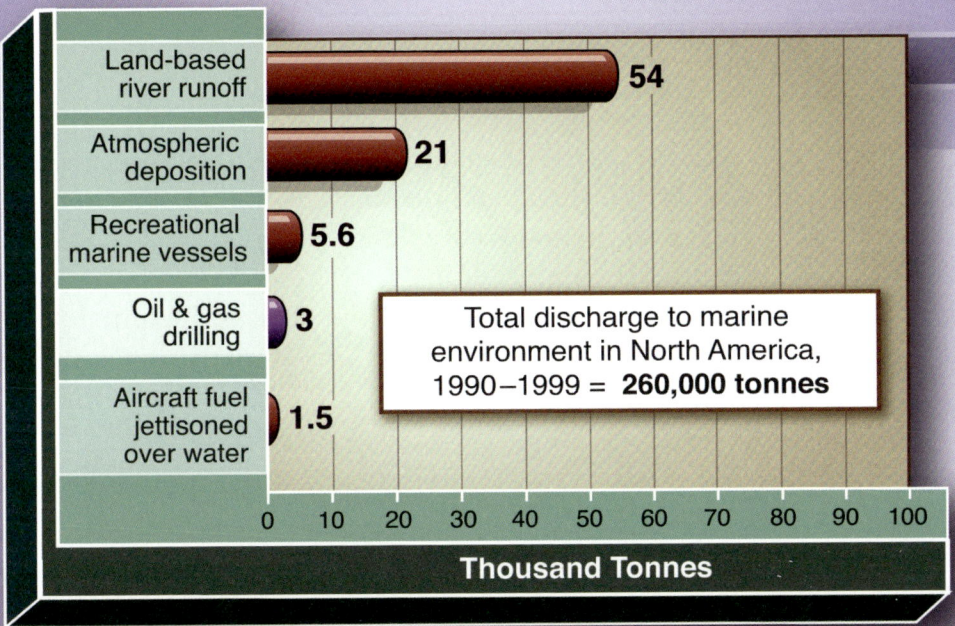

Taken from: National Research Council of the National Academies, *Oil in the Sea II: Inputs, Fates, and Effects*, Institute for Energy Research, October 21, 2010.

socioeconomic sensitivity adjustment factor of 2 raises those costs to $1.2 billion, and applying the EPA formula including the highest vulnerability (wildlife) and habitat sensitivity factor (wetlands) raises those costs to nearly $1 billion, for a total of $2.2 billion.

This figure is basically the same as the total clean up costs of the biggest oil spill in U.S. history: In 1989, the *Exxon Valdez* oil tanker leaked 250,000 barrels of crude oil (about 10 million gallons) after being run aground on a reef in Alaska's Prince William Sound. The

BP blowout will eclipse the *Exxon Valdez* spill if it continues flowing for another 33 days. The ultimate clean up costs for the *Exxon Valdez* accident amounted to about $2.2 billion, with additional legal costs and damage payments of $2.3 billion. Some analysts are estimating that the costs for clean up and payment for economic losses from the BP spill might reach as high as $12.5 billion. As it should be, BP's corporate leadership has declared that the company will be responsible for paying for the costs of the spill.

A Risk Worth Taking

In his book, *Normal Accidents: Living with High Risk Technologies* (1984), Yale University sociologist Charles Perrow noted that when a technology fails, it often does so because "the problem is just something that never occurred to the designers." Assuming no malfeasance, whatever went wrong with the *Deepwater Horizon* drill rig will likely uncover just such a problem and future designers will fix it. Progress is a trial and error process and increasing safety results from learning how to make better trade-offs over time between risks. Despite this current disaster, offshore oil drilling remains a risk well worth taking.

> **EVALUATING THE AUTHOR'S ARGUMENTS:**
>
> Ronald Bailey suggests that whatever problem caused the *Deepwater Horizon* to explode and spill oil into the Gulf of Mexico in 2010 is likely be fixed by future engineers, making offshore oil drilling safer and even more beneficial. What do you think? Do you agree that the risk of future oil spills is likely to go down? If so, why? If not, why not? Cite evidence from the texts you have read in your answer.

Chapter 3

How Should Humans Respond to Species Decline?

Across the globe, from Indonesia to the United States, people are organizing to protect endangered species.

Viewpoint 1

The Endangered Species Act Is Effective

National Wildlife Federation

> "The Endangered Species Act is very important, because it saves our native fish, plants and wildlife from going extinct."

The National Wildlife Federation (NWF) is America's largest conservation organization. It partners with more than 4 million supporters who work together to protect species and restore wildlife habitat. In the following viewpoint the NWF argues that the Endangered Species Act (ESA) is a critical tool for protecting species and habitat. The organization asserts that since its creation in 1973, the ESA has been used to protect thousands of plants and animals and even bring some of these back from the brink of extinction. Wolves, birds, bears, and panthers are just a few of the animals that have benefited from protection under the act. The NWF contends that when a species is lost, the effects are often devastating and ripple throughout the entire ecosystem. Protecting all plant and animal species from extinction is therefore an important activity, it maintains, that benefits both people and the environment.

National Wildlife Federation, "Endangered Species Act," 2010. www.nwf.org/Wildlife/Wildlife-Conservation/Understanding-Wildlife-conservation/Endangered-Species-Act.aspx. Reproduced by permission of National Wildlife Federation.

AS YOU READ, CONSIDER THE FOLLOWING QUESTIONS:
1. What criteria are evaluated when a species is being considered for the Endangered Species List, according to the National Wildlife Federation?
2. What does the term *take* mean in the context of the viewpoint?
3. In what way has the Endangered Species Act helped gray wolves, according to the author?

The Endangered Species Act (ESA for short) was enacted by Congress in 1973. Under the ESA, the federal government has the responsibility to protect:

- Endangered Species—species that are likely to become extinct throughout all or a large portion of their range.
- Threatened Species—species that are likely to become endangered in the near future.
- Critical habitat—vital to the survival of endangered or threatened species.

The Endangered Species Act has lists of protected plant and animal species both nationally and worldwide. When a species is given ESA protection, it is said to be a "listed" species.

As of October 2009, 1,361 plants and animals in the United States were listed as threatened or endangered. There are many additional species that are currently being evaluated for possible protection under the ESA, and they are called "candidate" species.

How the Endangered Species Act Works

Under the Endangered Species Act, the U.S. Fish and Wildlife Service oversees the listing and protection of all terrestrial animals and plants as well as freshwater fish. The National Marine Fisheries Service oversees marine fish and wildlife.

When the U.S. Fish and Wildlife Service or the National Marine Fisheries Service is investigating the health of a species, they look at scientific data collected by local, state and national scientists.

In order to be listed as a candidate, a species has to be found to qualify for protected status under the Endangered Species Act.

Whether or not a species is listed as endangered or threatened then depends on a number of factors, including the urgency and whether adequate protections exist through other means.

When deciding whether a species should be added to the Endangered Species List, the following criteria are evaluated:

- Has a large percentage of the species' vital habitat been degraded or destroyed?
- Has the species been over-consumed by commercial, recreational, scientific or educational uses?
- Is the species threatened by disease or predation?
- Do current regulations or legislations inadequately protect the species?
- Are there other manmade factors that threaten the long-term survival of the species?

If scientific research reveals that the answer to one or more of the above questions is yes, then the species can be listed under the Endangered Species Act.

What Does Endangered Species Act Protection Mean?

Once a species becomes listed as "endangered" or "threatened," it receives special protections by the federal government. Animals are protected from "take" and being traded or sold. A listed plant is protected if on federal property or if federal actions are involved, such as the issuing of a federal permit on private land.

The term "take" is used in the Endangered Species Act to include, "harass, harm, pursue, hunt, shoot, wound, kill, trap, capture, or collect, or to attempt to engage in any such conduct." The law also protects against interfering in vital breeding and behavioral activities or degrading critical habitat.

The Importance of Protecting Threatened and Endangered Species

The primary goal of the Endangered Species Act is to make species' populations healthy and vital so they can be delisted from the Endangered Species Act. The U.S. Fish and Wildlife Service and the National Marine Fisheries Service actively invest time and resources to bringing endangered or threatened species back from the brink of extinction.

The Endangered Species Act is very important, because it saves our native fish, plants and wildlife from going extinct. Once they are gone, they are gone forever and there is no going back. Losing even a single species can have disastrous impacts on the rest of the ecosystem, because the effects will be felt throughout the food chain.

From providing cures to deadly diseases to maintaining natural ecosystems and improving overall quality of life, the benefits of preserving threatened and endangered species are invaluable.

Six Success Stories

Bald Eagle. In the 1960s, a mere 500 bald eagles could be found soaring across America's lower 48 states. Dangerous pesticides and chemicals, released into bald eagle habitats, thinned the shells of their

When the Endangered Species Act of 1973 was enacted, the American bald eagle was in danger of extinction. In a July 1999 White House ceremony, President Bill Clinton announced that the bald eagle had made a recovery and was being removed from the endangered species list.

eggs, killing their young. By the late 1960's, only 400 breeding pairs of bald eagles were found in the lower 48 states. The outlook was not good for our national symbol. Thanks to the protections afforded by the Endangered Species Act, bald eagle numbers have rebounded to more than 7,000 breeding pairs of bald eagles today. Captive breeding programs, habitat protection, and a ban on [the pesticide] DDT contributed to the successful recovery of this American symbol. The species has made an astounding comeback thanks to the amazing work of American citizens, businesses, scientists and the U.S. government. These diverse groups came together to help protect bald eagles under the authority of the U.S. Endangered Species Act.

> **FAST FACT**
> At the time of its listing as endangered under the Endangered Species Act of 1973, the once-common gray wolf had been eliminated from its historic ranges in the Rocky Mountains and eastern United States. Thanks to protection from unregulated hunting and trapping and to reintroduction programs, notably in Yellowstone National Park, more than five thousand gray wolves now live in the lower forty-eight states.

Florida Panther. A 1989 census indicated that the Florida panther population had dropped to between 30 to 50 individuals. This decline was the result of habitat loss, degradation and fragmentation. Today, the species population is still below 100 individuals, but without Endangered Species Act protections the panther would likely be extinct. These protections include captive breeding, habitat protection, wildlife underpass construction and the introduction of Texas cougars to prevent inbreeding.

Gray Wolf. Gray wolves once ranged across the entire North American continent. However, as a result of poisoning and trapping by ranchers, farmers and government agents, by the mid-20th century, only a few hundred of the species remained in the entire lower 48 states. Today, thanks to Endangered Species Act protections, more than 2,500 wolves reside in Minnesota, roughly 500 wolves in Wisconsin and Michigan and another 500 individuals in western states. The gray wolf's success is a result of Endangered Species Act–

"Eagle Soar Fourth," cartoon by Jeff Parker and PoliticalCartoons.com, July 2, 2007. Copyright © 2007 Jeff Parker, Florida Today, and PoliticalCartoons.com. All rights reserved.

stimulated efforts such as public education about the species, habitat restoration, wolf introduction into various areas and compensation of ranchers for livestock killed by wolves.

Grizzly Bear. Within the lower 48 states, grizzly bear populations have been reduced to a mere two percent of their former range due to a combination of excessive hunting, conversion of habitat to human uses and fragmentation of habitat caused by such things as extensive networks of logging roads. Grizzly bears were brought under federal management when they were listed under the Endangered Species Act in 1975. At that time fewer than 250 bears occupied the Yellowstone area. Since then, the coordinated efforts of state and federal agencies, conservation organizations and private citizens have increased this population to more than 600 bears. In addition to the Yellowstone grizzlies, approximately 600 bears occupy habitat in the lower 48 states, including portions of Glacier National Park and adjacent areas in Montana and in northern Washington adjacent to the Canadian border.

Peregrine Falcon. A 1964 survey found that peregrine falcons did not inhabit a single cliff in the eastern United States or Canadian maritime provinces. By 1970, a mere 10 to 20 percent of the historical falcon population remained, due to egg and nestling collection, intentional shooting and DDT use. Endangered Species Act protections for the falcon included captive breeding, preventing human disturbances to nesting and protection and enhancement of critical breeding and wintering habitat. As a result, populations are thriving. The species was delisted in 1999 and today there are more than 1,400 breeding pairs of peregrines in North America.

Red-Cockaded Woodpecker. In the 1960s, a study predicted that the red-cockaded woodpecker would become extinct due to logging, deforestation and fire suppression. Fewer than 15,000 of these birds survive in about one percent of its former range. Thanks to the Act, restrictions were placed on habitat destruction and since 1995, more than 500,000 acres of private lands have been enrolled in conservation programs, leading the woodpecker toward recovery.

EVALUATING THE AUTHOR'S ARGUMENTS:

In this viewpoint the National Wildlife Federation uses facts, statistics, examples, and reasoning to make the argument that the Endangered Species Act is important and effective. The author does not, however, use any quotations supporting this position. If you were to rewrite this article and insert quotations, what authorities might you quote? Where would you place the quotations, and why?

Viewpoint 2

The Endangered Species Act Is Not Effective

PR Newswire

"The [Endangered Species] Act severely penalized landowners, and as a result, many fearful property owners . . . make their land inhospitable to endangered species."

In the following viewpoint PR Newswire, releasing information from the National Center for Policy Analysis, argues that the Endangered Species Act (ESA) does more harm than good to the plants and animals under its protection. The author expresses the position of analyst Brian Seasholes that the ESA imposes tight regulations on lands where endangered species live. This ends up punishing the landowner for inadvertently harboring endangered species. As a result, landowners have gone out of their way to make their land uninhabitable by the endangered species, which is counterproductive and benefits neither animals nor people. They conclude that conservation efforts should reward, rather than punish, landowners for participating in the conservation of species.

Seaholes, who is quoted heavily in this viewpoint, writes frequently on several issues related to wildlife, including land use and property rights, community-based

PR Newswire, "Endangered Species Act Does More Harm Than Good: Land-Use Controls Punishes Landowners and Animals Alike, Says NCPA Study," September 25, 2007. Copyright © 2011 PR Newswire Association LLC. All Rights Reserved. Reproduced by permission.

conservation, and the Endangered Species Act. The National Center for Policy Analysis is a nonprofit, nonpartisan research institute that advocates private solutions to public policy problems. PR Newswire is the leading global vendor in information and news distribution services for professional communicators.

AS YOU READ, CONSIDER THE FOLLOWING QUESTIONS:
1. According to the author, what use restrictions does the Endangered Species Act impose on public and private lands?
2. How much does the author say that government pays landowners for restricting use of land for an endangered species?
3. In what two ways does Brian Seaholes say the Endangered Species Act might better protect species?

The Endangered Species Act, which was created to help protect species in danger of extinction, put the very species it is supposed to protect at risk, according to a new study by the National Center for Policy Analysis (NCPA). The Act severely penalized landowners, and as a result, many fearful property owners have taken action to make their land inhospitable to endangered species.

"The Endangered Species Act has wreaked havoc on wildlife and landowners," said NCPA Adjunct Scholar Brian Seaholes, who authored the study. "The ESA punishes landowners for harboring endangered species, and the tragic result has been a scorched earth policy towards the very species the Act is supposed to protect."

According to Seaholes, the greatest problem with the Act is its land-use control provisions. These provisions penalize public and private landowners by:

- Prohibiting, or tightly regulating, any activity considered to be a danger to the species, such as farming, lumbering, construction, human habitation or even visiting the land.
- Providing no compensation to the land owner for the loss of land value, loss of income or lost use of land.

- Subjecting millions of acres to land use regulations for a single protected species.

"If one had deliberately written legislation to harm endangered species, it would be almost impossible to top the ESA," said Seasholes. "The only way to reverse this is to remove the penalties."

Seasholes notes there are two examples that point the way toward an Endangered Species Act that would better protect species:

- The U.S. has a long and proud tradition of private wildlife conservation that has saved such species as the plains bison.
- Much of the rest of the world, led by a number of countries in Southern Africa, have turned away from the punitive approach to wildlife conservation because they have realized that punishing people for harboring wildlife is the surest way to ensure that wildlife declines.

"Most of the world has learned what the Endangered Species Act's supporters refuse to acknowledge," said Seasholes. "Effective wildlife conservation depends first on not punishing the people who bear the costs of harboring wildlife. When the ESA's penalties are removed, then a wide range of incentives can be employed and the dormant goodwill and creativity of America's landowners will flourish."

The NCPA is an internationally known nonprofit, nonpartisan research institute with offices in Dallas and Washington, D. C. that advocates private solutions to public policy problems. We depend on the contributions of individuals, corporations and foundations that share our mission. The NCPA accepts no government grants.

> **FAST FACT**
>
> Only 48 of the 2,014 threatened or endangered plants and animals listed under the Endangered Species Act (ESA) have been removed from the list. According to environmental writer Jonathan DuHamel, 18 of those 48 were removed for mistakes in original data, 9 became extinct, and the rest recovered for reasons unrelated to the ESA, such as the banning of the pesticide DDT.

EVALUATING THE AUTHOR'S ARGUMENTS:

Compare this viewpoint, which discusses an NCPA study by Brian Seasholes arguing that the Endangered Species Act has done more harm than good, with the previous viewpoint by the National Wildlife Federation, which supports the Endangered Species Act. With which viewpoint do you more strongly agree? Support your answer with evidence from one or both viewpoints.

Viewpoint 3

The Giant Panda Should Be Left to Go Extinct

Chris Packham

"Maybe if we took all the cash we spend on pandas and just bought rainforest with it, we might be doing a better job."

In the following viewpoint Chris Packham explains why he believes efforts to save the giant panda from extinction are misguided and a waste of resources. The panda is a naturally weak animal, he contends, and suggests that it may have simply run its natural course on earth. Packham accepts that death is a part of life and that extinction is a sometimes necessary evolutionary reality. Strong species overtake weak species, which cannot necessarily be protected. Packham concludes that conservation dollars are limited and it would be better to spend them saving large swaths of habitat or creatures that have a better chance of surviving.

Packham is a wildlife expert, photographer, author, and cohost of *Autumnwatch*, a British nature show.

Chris Packham, "Should Pandas Be Left to Face Extinction?," *The Guardian*, September 23, 2009. Guardian.co.uk. Copyright © 2009 by Guardian News & Media Ltd. All rights reserved. Reproduced by permission.

AS YOU READ, CONSIDER THE FOLLOWING QUESTIONS:
1. What is "single-species conservation" and what is Packham's opinion of it?
2. What natural weaknesses does the panda have that Packham says make it vulnerable to extinction? Name at least two.
3. What is the Yangtze River dolphin and how does it factor into the author's argument?

I don't want the panda to die out. I want species to stay alive—that's why I get up in the morning. I don't even kill mosquitoes or flies. So if pandas can survive, that would be great. But let's face it: conservation, both nationally and globally, has a limited amount of resources, and I think we're going to have to make some hard, pragmatic choices.

It Costs Too Much to Save Pandas

The truth is, pandas are extraordinarily expensive to keep going. We spend millions and millions of pounds [Sterling] on pretty much this one species, and a few others, when we know that the best thing we could do would be to look after the world's biodiversity hotspots with greater care. Without habitat, you've got nothing. So maybe if we took all the cash we spend on pandas and just bought rainforest with it, we might be doing a better job.

> **FAST FACT**
>
> *National Geographic* magazine estimates that it costs a zoo in the United States $2.6 million a year to host giant pandas. The cost tops $3 million a year if a panda gives birth.

Of course, it's easier to raise money for something fluffy. Charismatic megafauna like the panda do appeal to people's emotional side, and attract a lot of public attention. They are emblematic of what I would call single-species conservation: ie a focus on one animal. This approach began in the 1970s with Save the Tiger, Save the Panda, Save the Whale, and so on, and it is now out of date. I think pandas have had a valuable role in raising the profile of conservation, but perhaps "had" is the right word.

Extinction Is a Natural Part of Life

Panda conservationists may stand up and say, "It's a flagship species. We're also conserving Chinese forest, where there is a whole plethora of other things." And when that works, I'm not against it. But we have to accept that some species are stronger than others. The panda is a species of bear that has gone herbivorous and eats a type of food that isn't all that nutritious, and that dies out sporadically. It is susceptible to various diseases, and, up until recently, it has been almost impossible to breed in captivity. They've also got a very restricted range, which is ever decreasing, due to encroachment on their habitat by the Chinese population. Perhaps the panda was already destined to run out of time.

Extinction is very much a part of life on earth. And we are going to have to get used to it in the next few years because climate change

Chinese workers gather the massive amount of bamboo needed to feed pandas at a panda research institution in China. The world's captive panda population costs millions of dollars in feed-related expenditures.

Pandas Are Expensive to Exhibit

Giant pandas are on display in just four American zoos, in part because they are very expensive to keep. Hosting giant pandas costs a zoo an average of $2.6 million per year, more if they have cubs. A 2009 study found that over a three-year period, American zoos collectively spent $33 million more on pandas than they received in revenue exhibiting them.

Taken from: Lynne Warren, "Panda, Inc." *National Geographic*, July 2006; D'vera Cohn, "Zoos Find Pandas Don't Make the Cash to Cover Their Keep," *Washington Post*, August 7, 2005.

is going to result in all sorts of disappearances. The last large mammal extinction was another animal in China—the Yangtze river dolphin, which looked like a worn-out piece of pink soap with piggy eyes and was never going to make it on to anyone's T-shirt. If that had appeared beautiful to us, then I doubt very much that it would be extinct. But it vanished, because it was pig-ugly and swam around in a river where no one saw it. And now, sadly, it has gone for ever.

Focus on Areas of High Biodiversity

I'm not trying to play God; I'm playing God's accountant. I'm saying we won't be able to save it all, so let's do the best we can. And at the moment I don't think our strategies are best placed to do that. We should be focusing our conservation endeavours on biodiversity hotspots, spreading our net more widely and looking at good-quality habitat maintenance to preserve as much of the life as we possibly can, using hard science to make educated decisions as to which species are essential to a community's maintenance. It may well be that we can lose the cherries from the cake. But you don't want to lose the substance. Save the Rainforest, or Save the Kalahari: that would be better.

> **EVALUATING THE AUTHOR'S ARGUMENTS:**
>
> Chris Packham is a naturalist and conservationist. Does it surprise you, then, given his environmental background, that he would argue against doing everything possible to save an endangered animal like the giant panda? Why or why not? Explain your answer and then state whether or not you agree with him that the panda should be left to go extinct.

Viewpoint 4

The Giant Panda Should Not Be Left to Go Extinct

Simon Usborne

"Since when was it OK to 'pull the plug' on one of the world's most recognisable and best loved animals?"

Simon Usborne is a reporter for the British newspaper *The Independent*. In the following viewpoint he argues that giant pandas are worthy of conservation efforts. He explains that pandas are sensitive animals that are under multiple threats. Usborne thinks they are worth saving because they share habitat with other important species, they are an important Chinese icon, they have unique scientific and evolutionary value, and they are cute and popular. Usborne rejects the notion that people should pick which animals to save and which to let die out. If humans are responsible for causing the decline of a particular species, he argues, then they also have the responsibility to direct time, effort, and money to saving it.

AS YOU READ, CONSIDER THE FOLLOWING QUESTIONS:
1. What other animals does Usborne say benefit from panda protection efforts?
2. How does the author describe "panda diplomacy"?
3. What does Usborne say makes pandas evolutionarily unique?

Simon Usborne, "Hands Off the Pandas," *Independent* (London), September 23, 2009. Copyright © 2009 Independent News & Media PLC. All rights reserved. Reproduced by permission.

Poor Yang Yang and Kou Kou and Lun Lun. Chris Packham thinks you and all your panda friends are good-for-nothing, bamboo-munching, taxidermist-dodging benefit cheats. In an interview with *Radio Times*, . . . the BBC nature presenter launches a vicious assault on the embattled species. He says the giant panda has "gone down an evolutionary cul-de-sac". He adds: "It's not a strong species . . . I reckon we should pull the plug. Let them go with a degree of dignity".

And it gets worse. Last year [2008] the birdwatcher even threatened to "eat the last panda if I could have the money we've spent on panda conservation to [spend on] more sensible things". Eat a panda? What are you saying, Chris? Why not polish off a blue whale? You've got the mouth for it.

Panda Protection Helps Other Animals

Packham is right in one regard—the panda is under threat and often seems hopeless. Habitat loss, poaching and the bear's notorious disinterest in making baby pandas has left it clinging to life in isolated mountain ranges. There are fewer than 2,000 pandas in the wild, around 250 in captivity.

But since when was it OK to "pull the plug" on one of the world's most recognisable and best loved animals? . . .

Giant pandas belong to a select breed of animals qualifying as "charismatic megafauna". They are the poster boys of the natural world—the "T-shirt" animals whose plight is elevated to get us moist-eyed and agitated. "But pandas didn't ask to be cute and cuddly", says Mark Wright, the science adviser at WWF [World Wildlife Fund] (which has a panda for a logo). "The point is that by saving the panda you are saving the

> **FAST FACT**
>
> Aside from its value as a cultural icon, the giant panda plays a crucial role in its bamboo forest ecosystem by spreading seeds that increase vegetation, the World Wildlife Fund reports. If the giant panda goes extinct, other rare species in this ecosystem, such as the red panda, golden monkey, and crested ibis may be lost, too.

Shrinking Habitat, Shrinking Panda Population

According to the World Wildlife Fund, less than 2,500 adult pandas exist in the world.

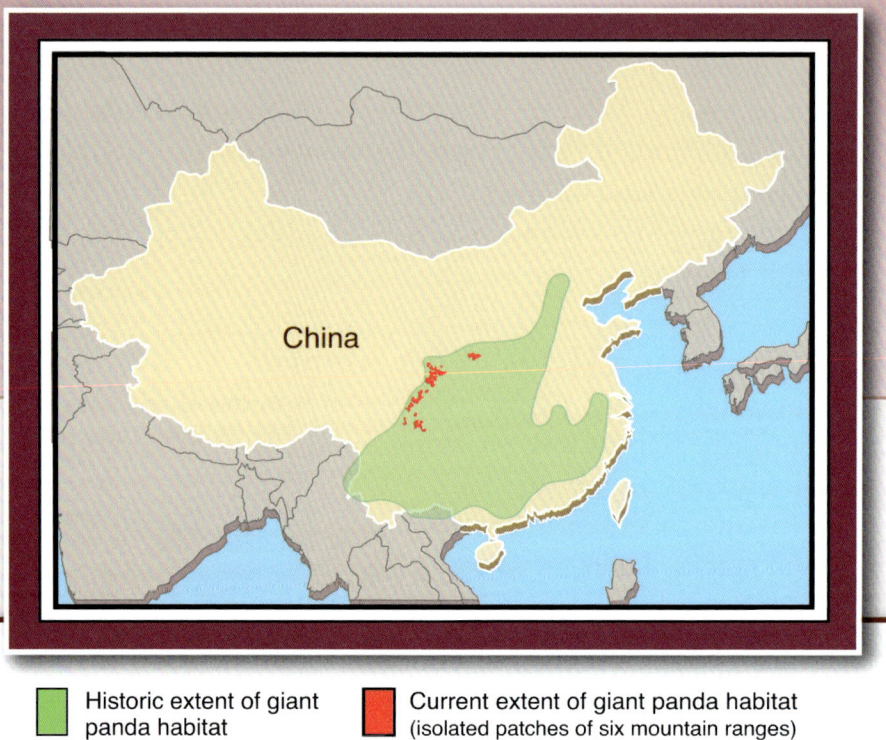

Historic extent of giant panda habitat

Current extent of giant panda habitat (isolated patches of six mountain ranges)

Taken from: China Highlights, Giant Panda Maps, March 3, 2011. www.chinahighlights.com/giant-panda/map.htm.

dozens of other endangered species that are unique to those habitats". So if we did pull the plug on the panda and its habitat, Wright says, we'd also kiss goodbye to the Sichuan wood owl and the Snowy-cheeked laughing thrush. And they're birds, Chris—you like birds.

There is no animal the Chinese love more, besides the mythical dragon, than the giant panda. They're called "di xiong mao", which means "big bear cat" and serve as a symbol of national pride. The animal appears on commemorative coins and Jing Jing the panda was one of Beijing's mascots, elected by Chinese voters, at last year's [2008's] Olympics. The panda is seen as a manifestation of the Yin and Yang philosophy of Chinese society. Their black and white coats and placid nature are held up as examples of harmony. And they have practical value. "Panda diplomacy" has helped Beijing build bridges, most recently with, Taiwan, usually by loaning [the] animals to zoos.

Pandas Are Vital to Science and People

There are two kinds of animals of interest to scientists—common ones (think flies) and the rare ones that may hold valuable secrets. "Pandas are famous in evolutionary science because they developed out of their wrist a unique appendage that works as a specialist thumb for stripping bamboo", says Bill Sutherland, a professor of conservation biology at Cambridge University. All too often lessons from nature die with endangered species. The gastric-brooding frog incubated its eggs in its stomach. Scientists seeking a cure for gastric ulcers were studying the acid-proof substance that protected those eggs until the frog became extinct. "You never know why or when a species will become vital to science", says Sutherland.

The panda's future isn't only important for the species who share its home. Pandas have become rare largely thanks to human encroachment. Vast tracts of south-east China have been deforested or given over to agriculture as China tries to fuel and feed a rapidly-growing population. Pandas are now one of the most protected species on the planet. The Wolong National Nature Reserve in Sichuan Province is one example. It is home to 150 pandas—and thousands of people. "Most of them derive a living from the panda", says Iain Valentine of Edinburgh Zoo. "They depend on pandas thriving".

Pandas Are Popular

Packham may say it's the panda's doe-eyed tranquillity and teddy-bear features that have skewed our perspective—but there's no denying the bear's cuteness. It turns out there's science behind our soppiness. The Austrian zoologist, Konrad Lorenz, argued that humans react positively to animals that resemble babies, because we have evolved instinctively to care for our offspring. So humans are genetically disposed to animals with big eyes and heads and cute little ears.

The arrival in April 2011 of a female giant panda at a Tokyo zoo caused a public sensation. Because pandas are considered to be the endangered species "poster-child," their conservation may lead to the conservation of other species.

If evidence of this theory were needed, visit YouTube and search for "sneezing baby panda". The clip, which has been seen 40 million times, shows a mother jumping out of her fur when her offspring interrupts teatime with an almighty sneeze. Packham either hasn't seen it or doesn't have a heart.

EVALUATING THE AUTHOR'S ARGUMENTS:

The author of this viewpoint, Simon Usborne, and Chris Packham, who authored the previous viewpoint, disagree on whether people should continue to try to save the panda from extinction. Which author do you think made the stronger argument? List at least three pieces of evidence that caused you to side with one of them.

Facts About Endangered Species

Extinction is a normal part of evolution; scientists estimate that 99 percent of all the species that have ever lived on earth have gone extinct. The current rate of extinction, however, is estimated to be a thousand times faster than the expected "background" rate of one extinction per million species per year.

According to the US Fish & Wildlife Service:
- 1,966 plants and animals are listed as endangered or threatened, including:
- 579 US animals
- 792 US plants
- 592 foreign animals
- 3 foreign plants

Animals once listed as endangered or threatened under the US Endangered Species Act but since delisted as recovered species include:
- the bald eagle
- the American alligator
- the American and Arctic peregrine falcons
- the red kangaroo
- the gray whale

The International Union for Conservation of Nature (IUCN) Red List is the world's most comprehensive inventory of endangered and threatened species. As of October 2010, the Red List had evaluated 55,926 of the world's 1,727,708 known species and assigned them to one of seven conservation status categories: Extinct, Extinct in the Wild, Critically Endangered, Endangered, Vulnerable, Near Threatened, or Least Concern.

According to the IUCN:
- One-fifth of the world's mammals, birds, amphibians, reptiles, and fishes are in imminent danger of extinction. That corresponds to:

- 25 percent of mammals
- 13 percent of birds
- 22 percent of reptiles
- 15 percent of fishes

Amphibians are the group at highest risk: 41 percent of amphibian species worldwide face extinction.

According to the World Wildlife Fund, the ten most critically endangered species are the:
- tiger
- polar bear
- Pacific walrus
- Magellanic penguin
- leatherback turtle
- bluefin tuna
- mountain gorilla
- monarch butterfly
- Javan rhinoceros
- giant panda

The Wildlife Conservation Society named the following to its 2010–2011 list of the most critically endangered species:
- Cuban crocodile
- Grenada dove
- Florida bonneted bat
- green-eyed frog
- Hunter's hartebeest
- ploughshare tortoise
- island gray fox
- Sumatran orangutan
- vaquita (a small porpoise)
- white-headed langur (a monkey)

Some of the many benefits of biodiversity include:
- maintaining soil and water quality
- limiting the spread of disease
- waste decomposition

- pollination and seed spread
- providing sources of medicines
- genetic health of crop species

The main threats to biodiversity and endangered species include:
- habitat destruction
- overhunting and overfishing
- invasive alien species
- pollution
- overpopulation
- climate change

Southeast Asia is experiencing the most dramatic declines in biodiversity, largely because of habitat destruction, especially deforestation to produce tropical hardwood for export and to clear land for oil palm plantations.

The Intergovernmental Panel on Climate Change (IPCC) forecasts a global rise in temperature of 1.8 to 6.4 degrees Celsius by 2100, very likely due to increases in greenhouse gases caused by human activities such as the burning of fossil fuels. Some of the impacts of climate change likely to push endangered species closer to extinction are:
- shrinking of glaciers and Arctic and Antarctic sea ice, with likely disappearance of summer sea ice in the Arctic by 2050
- increased drought and desertification
- coastal flooding and erosion

According to the IPCC:
- Increases in sea surface temperature of 1–3 degrees Celsius would likely lead to widespread destruction of the world's coral reefs.
- If the global average temperature rise is more than 3.5 degrees Celsius (6.3 degrees Fahrenheit), there will be global species extinction rates of 40–70 percent.

American Opinions About Endangered Species

Polls taken by *Newsweek* in 2000 and again in 2007 asked Americans what they think is the most important environmental problem facing the world. Responses in 2007 included the following:

- 38 percent said global warming (12 percent said this in 2000)
- 14 percent said water pollution (19 percent said this in 2000)
- 13 percent said air pollution (19 percent said this in 2000)
- 10 percent said garbage and landfills (17 percent said this in 2000)
- 7 percent said loss of the ozone layer (13 percent said this in 2000)
- 3 percent said endangered or vanishing species (5 percent said this in 2000)
- 1 percent said acid rain (3 percent said this in 2000)
- 7 percent said it was some other problem (4 percent said this in 2000)
- 7 percent said they were unsure (8 percent said this in 2000)

A 2002 Fox News/Opinion Dynamics poll asked Americans whether they thought it was ever acceptable to use cloning and found that the majority did not think it was acceptable to clone endangered or extinct species:

- 29 percent said it was acceptable to clone endangered species
- 64 percent said it was not
- 7 percent were unsure
- 20 percent said it was acceptable to clone extinct species
- 72 percent said it was not
- 8 percent were unsure

Organizations to Contact

The editors have compiled the following list of organizations concerned with the issues debated in this book. The descriptions are derived from materials provided by the organizations. All have publications or information available for interested readers. The list was compiled on the date of publication of the present volume; the information provided here may change. Be aware that many organizations take several weeks or longer to respond to inquiries, so allow as much time as possible for the receipt of requested materials.

African Wildlife Foundation (AWF)
1400 Sixteenth St. NW, Ste. 120, Washington, DC 20036
(202) 939-3333 • toll free: (888) 494-5354
e-mail: africanwildlife@awf.org
website: www.awf.org

The AWF, founded in 1961, works to conserve Africa's endangered species (public awareness campaigns focus on large mammals) through parks, preserves, and projects such as the African Heartlands Program, International Gorilla Conservation Program, Mweka College of African Wildlife Management, and the Kenyan Ecolodge Sanctuary at 01 Lentille in Laikipia, Kenya. The foundation publishes the quarterly e-newsletter *African Wildlife News*; its website offers an educational wildlife photo gallery, interactive maps, fact sheets such as "Land and Habitat Conservation," and news articles.

American Livestock Breeds Conservancy (ALBC)
PO Box 477, Pittsboro, NC 27312
(919) 542-5704
e-mail: albc@albc-usa.org
website: www.albc-usa.org

The ALBC works to prevent the extinction of rare breeds of American livestock. The conservancy believes that conservation is necessary to protect the genetic range and survival ability of these species. The

ALBC provides general information about the importance of saving rare breeds as well as specific guidelines for individuals interested in raising rare breeds.

American Zoo and Aquarium Association (AZA)
8403 Colseville Rd., Ste. 710, Silver Spring, MD 20910
website: www.aza.org

AZA represents over 160 zoos and aquariums in North America. The association provides information on captive breeding of endangered species, conservation education, natural history, and wildlife legislation. AZA publications include the *Species Survival Plans* and the *Annual Report on Conservation and Science*.

Census of Marine Life (COML)
Consortium for Ocean Leadership
1201 New York Ave. NW, Ste. 420, Washington, DC 20005
(202) 332-0063
e-mail: coml@oceanleadership.org
website: www.coml.org

Released in 2010, the COML is a ten-year joint effort of more than twenty-seven hundred scientists in eighty countries to compile the most comprehensive inventory of marine life ever attempted. COML expeditions have documented more than 250,000 species, including 1,200 formerly unknown species. The census has also documented widespread declines in marine populations and issued a range of policy recommendations to halt further decline. Available on its website are COML findings, cutting-edge research tools, and image and video galleries that offer a look into how modern fisheries, offshore oil drilling, waste disposal, and climate change are affecting marine plants and animals.

Convention on International Trade in Endangered Species of Wild Fauna and Flora (CITES)
International Environment House, Chemin des Anémones, CH-1219 Chatelaine, Geneva, Switzerland
+41 22-917-81-39/40
e-mail: info@cites.org
website: www.cites.org

CITES is an international agreement among governments, currently of 175 countries, committed to ensure that the international trade in specimens of wild animals and plants does not threaten their survival. Since the agreement went into effect in 1975, all import and export of covered species must be authorized through a licensing system; covered species are listed on one of three appendices according to the degree of protection they need. Available on the CITES website are the full appendices, the latest listing and delisting decisions and export quotas, and a glossary of often-used terms. A wide variety of publications include national reports, the e-book for laypersons *The Evolution of CITES*, and the biannual newsletter *CITES World*.

Endangered Species Coalition (ESC)
PO Box 65195
Washington, DC 20035
(240) 353-2765
e-mail: esc@stopextinction.org
website: www.stopextinction.org

The ESC is composed of conservation, professional, and animal-welfare groups that work to extend the Endangered Species Act and to ensure its enforcement. The ESC encourages public activism through grassroots organizations, direct lobbying, and letter-writing and telephone campaigns. Its publications include the book *The Endangered Species Act: A Commitment Worth Keeping* and numerous articles, fact sheets, position papers, and bill summaries regarding the Endangered Species Act.

George C. Marshall Institute
1625 K St. NW, Ste. 1050, Washington, DC 20006
(202) 296-9655
e-mail: info@marshall.org
website: www.marshall.org

The George C. Marshall Institute, a nonprofit organization founded in 1984, takes a denialist minority position on global warming science. It argues that the scientific view of the causes and effects of global climate change, including the contribution of human activity and the danger to animal and plant species, is unproven and politicized. The institute publishes reports opposing restrictions on greenhouse gas emissions, including "Considering Climate and Energy Policy in 2011," physics professor William Happer's 2009 congressional testimony about the benefits of increased carbon dioxide in the atmosphere.

Intergovernmental Panel on Climate Change (IPCC)
IPCC Secretariat, c/o World Meteorological Organization
7 bis Avenue de la Paix
C.P. 2300, CH-1211, Geneva 2, Switzerland
+41 22-730-8208
e-mail: ipcc-sec@wmo.int
website: www.ipcc.ch

The IPCC, established in 1988 by the World Meteorological Organization and the United Nations Environment Programme, evaluates global climate change and the role of human activity in global warming based on accumulated international scientific evidence and peer-reviewed published findings. Recipient of the 2007 Nobel Peace Prize, the IPCC is widely cited as the world's foremost authority on the current status and likely effects of climate change. The *IPCC Fourth Assessment Report* (known as AR4), issued in 2007 and available in summary and full forms on the official website, is an urgent call to action. It concludes that global warming is undeniable; that it is due to greenhouse gas emissions caused by human activity; that atmospheric concentrations of carbon dioxide, nitrous oxide, and methane are far higher than they have been for 650,000 years; and that a "business as usual" response will lead to catastrophic species extinction.

International Fund for Animal Welfare (IFAW)
411 Main St., PO Box 193, Yarmouth Port, MA 02675
(508) 744-2000 • toll-free: (800) 932-4329
e-mail: info@ifaw.org
website: www.ifaw.org

The IFAW is a nonprofit animal advocacy organization founded in the 1970s to combat Canadian commercial white-coat harp seal hunting. Today it campaigns to protect animals that are domesticated as well as endangered in captivity or in the wild, around the world. Its website offers statistics and detailed description of dozens of targeted species and their habitats. The fund publishes annual reports, animal fact sheets, position papers, the quarterly *IFAW Newsletter*, and updates on current campaigns such as collaring elephants in Kenya, banning bear hunts in

Russia, and protecting animals in the aftermath of the 2011 Japanese earthquake and tsunami.

National Endangered Species Act Reform Coalition (NESARC)
1050 Thomas Jefferson St. NW, 6th Fl., Washington, DC 20007
(202) 333-7481
e-mail: nesarc@vnf.com
website: www.nesarc.org

NESARC is a coalition of roughly 150 member organizations, including rural irrigators, municipalities, farm bureaus, electric utilities, forestry companies, builders associations, and property owners. The coalition seeks legislative reform of what it views as overly restrictive, vague, and inflexible standards and requirements of the Endangered Species Act (ESA). NESARC calls for fair compensation and a greater decision-making role for private landowners whose property use and value is reduced by ESA restrictions and more stringent scientific evidence that ESA actions are warranted. The coalition issues biweekly updates and analysis of new regulations, white papers, legal briefs, and congressional hearing transcripts.

National Wildlife Federation (NWF)
11100 Wildlife Center Dr., Reston, VA 20190-5362
(800) 822-9919
website: www.nwf.org

The NWF is a nonprofit grassroots organization dedicated to habitat and wildlife conservation in the United States. Its current campaigns include cleanup of the Great Lakes and the Everglades, grasslands preservation, and wildlife rescue following the 2010 BP oil spill in the Gulf of Mexico. Several of its activities are geared for young people, including its magazines *National Wildlife, Ranger Rick, Your Big Backyard,* and *Wild Animal Baby;* its blogs *Green Hour* and *Wildlife Promise;* and its annual Connie Awards, recognizing individual effort in restoring wildlife habitat and conserving American wildlife.

Nature Conservancy
4245 N. Fairfax Dr., Ste. 100, Arlington, VA 22203-1606
(703) 841-5300 • toll-free: (800) 628-6860
website: www.nature.org

The Nature Conservancy is a leading national organization that identifies and preserves ecologically important habitat around the world through the key protection tools of land acquisition and so-called debt-for-nature swaps, by which a portion of a country's foreign debt is forgiven for setting aside land for conservation. Founded in 1951, the conservancy reports roughly a million members and the protection of 17 million acres (69,000 sq. km) in the United States and 117 million acres (473,000 sq. km) internationally. Its publications include the quarterly magazine *Nature Conservancy*, field guides, and the e-newsletter *Great Places*. The conservancy's website features the page "Our Science," updates on the research of more than five hundred staff scientists worldwide, and numerous links on issues such as ecotourism, invasive species, and rain forests.

Rainforest Action Network (RAN)
221 Pine St., 5th Fl., San Francisco, CA 94104
(415) 398-4404
e-mail: answers@ran.org
website: www.ran.org

RAN works to preserve the world's rain forests and protect the rights of native forest-dwelling peoples. The network sponsors letter-writing campaigns, boycotts, and demonstrations in response to environmental concerns. It publishes miscellaneous fact sheets, the monthly *Action Alert Bulletin*, and the quarterly *World Rainforest Report*.

The Rewilding Institute (TRI)
PO Box 13768, Albuquerque, NM 87192
e-mail: tri@rewilding.org
website: http://rewilding.org

TRI is a conservation think tank that advocates wildlife conservation on a continental scale. Its primary proposal is the scientifically credible, practically managed introduction of large carnivores such as lions, tigers, bears, and wolves into suitable habitat in North America, along with the creation of linked migration routes across the continent to allow animals' natural movement. TRI argues that humans and top predators once did and can again coexist in North America, and that without such a radical rewilding plan, dwindling populations of predator species in Africa and Asia are doomed. The institute's website offers abundant links to wildlands network design and carnivore protection sites and publications such as environmental activist founder Dave Foreman's book *Rewilding North America*.

US Fish and Wildlife Service (FWS)
Endangered Species Program
4401 N. Fairfax Dr., Rm. 420, Arlington, VA 22203
(703) 358-1949 • toll-free: (800) 344-WILD
website: www.fws.gov/endangered

The FWS, a division of the US Department of the Interior, manages the 150-million-acre National Wildlife Refuge System. It is one of two federal agencies responsible for administering and enforcing the Endangered Species Act and CITES, listing and delisting threatened and endangered animal and plant species, and compiling general statistics on the status of protected species such as migratory birds. It shares this responsibility with the National Oceanic and Atmospheric Administration's National Marine Fisheries Service. The FWS Endangered Species Program website publishes a wide variety of free factsheets, brochures, handbooks, and periodicals, including the quarterly *Endangered Species Bulletin*. Resources in the FWS Kids and Educators section include community service projects, photographs and videos, and the latest uses of GPS to track animal populations and invasive species.

Wildlands Network
PO Box 5284, Titusville, FL 32783
toll-free phone and fax: (877) 554-5234
e-mail: info@wildlandsnetwork.org
website: www.twp.org

Cofounded by conservation biologist Michael Soulé and fellow wilderness advocate Dave Foreman in 1991, the nonprofit, nonpartisan Wildlands Network maintains that habitat fragmentation caused by human development is causing critical biodiversity loss. Its mission is the restoration of endangered North American species and habitats, based on public- and private-sector cooperation in establishing a vast network of four connected wilderness areas, called wildways, that allow species to roam freely and safely across the continent. Detailed information on each wildway is available on the organization's website, along with articles and an e-newsletter.

International Union for Conservation of Nature (IUCN)
USA Multilateral Office
1630 Connecticut Ave. NW, 3rd Fl., Washington, DC 20009-1053

(202) 387-4826
e-mail: postmaster@iucnus.org
website: www.iucn.org

The IUCN is an important network of hundreds of governmental and nongovernmental agencies and thousands of scientists from 140 countries dedicated to preservation of biodiversity and ecologically sustainable use of natural resources. The union sponsors scientific research and congresses, coordinates resource management projects such as the global Water and Nature Initiative and Peace Parks, and investigates emergencies such as criminal poaching of critically endangered African rhinoceroses in 2011. Its primary publication is the annual *IUCN Red List*, the world's most authoritative inventory of endangered animal and plant species. The IUCN website offers an up-to-date news section; its publications catalog lists over three thousand documents, more than six hundred of which are free and downloadable.

World Wildlife Fund (WWF)
1250 Twenty-Fourth St. NW, PO Box 97180, Washington, DC 20090-7180
(202) 293-4800
e-mail: membership@wwfus.org
website: www.worldwildlife.org

The WWF, a charity founded in 1961, is the world's largest independent conservation organization, with 5 million supporters in more than ninety countries. It sponsors and runs more than a thousand field projects worldwide in the effort to halt and reverse the destruction of biodiversity and natural habitat. The WWF's work focuses on three biomes (forests, freshwater ecosystems, and oceans and coasts) and eight flagship species (giant pandas, tigers, whales, dolphins, rhinos, elephants, marine turtles, and great apes). The WWF publishes books on endangered wildlife, wild places, and global environmental challenges and the bimonthly newsletter *Focus*. A full bibliography of its conservation science articles, with abstracts, is available on its website, as are interactive maps, photo galleries, and links to current project sites.

For Further Reading

Books

Corwin, Jeff. *100 Heartbeats: The Race to Save Earth's Most Endangered Species.* Emmaus, PA: Rodale, 2009. The biologist, Emmy Award–winning producer, and TV host discusses polar and panda bears, Florida panthers, Bengal tigers, and other creatures in this look at endangered species and global efforts to save them.

Earle, Sylvia. *The World Is Blue: How Our Fate and the Ocean's Are One.* New York: National Geographic, 2010. Presents compelling personal stories to put the problems of the ocean and ocean life in perspective for a wide public audience.

Fraser, Caroline. *Rewilding the World: Dispatches from the Conservation Revolution.* New York: Picador, 2010. An inspiring story of what grassroots activism can achieve for endangered species and habitats.

Goodall, Jane, Thayne Maynard, and Gail Hudson. *Hope for Animals and Their World: How Endangered Species Are Being Rescued from the Brink.* New York: Grand Central, 2009. Offers good news on the endangered species front by chronicling the revival of six mammal and bird species, including Mongolian miniature horses and Australian wallabies, that became extinct in the wild but are being reintroduced to their natural habitat through captive breeding.

Levy, Sharon. *Once and Future Giants: What Ice Age Extinctions Tell Us About the Fate of Earth's Largest Animals.* New York: Oxford University Press, 2011. Examines the extent of human influence on megafauna extinctions past and present and explores innovative conservation efforts around the globe.

Sartore, Joel. *Rare: Portraits of America's Endangered Species.* New York: National Geographic/Focal Point, 2010. Chronicles a three-year investigation into the Endangered Species Act and the creatures it exists to protect through a series of stunning photographs.

Stolzenburg, William. *Where the Wild Things Were: Life, Death, and Ecological Wreckage in a Land of Vanishing Predators.* New York: Bloomsbury USA, 2009. A wildlife journalist examines predation's crucial role in the preservation of ecological diversity and paints a nightmarish picture of what happens to ecosystems when they lose their top predators.

Tobin, Mitch. *Endangered: Biodiversity on the Brink*. Golden, CO: Fulcrum, 2010. Explores the many problems animals and plants face around the world, including urban sprawl, wasteful water use, wildfires, extreme weather patterns, and examines whether the Endangered Species Act can prevent an extinction crisis.

Periodicals

Barnosky, Anthony D., et al. "Has the Earth's Sixth Mass Extinction Already Arrived?," *Nature*, March 3, 2011.

Buchen, Lizzie. "Are Efforts to Save the Panda a Giant Waste of Money?," *Discover*, August 12, 2008.

Coffey, Rebecca. "New Species: Found Today, Lost Tomorrow," *Discover*, January/February 2011.

Eveleth, Rose. "Zoo Illogical: Ugly Animals Need Protection from Extinction, Too," *Scientific American*, December 8, 2010.

Glover, Katherine. "All Worked UP," *Sierra Club Magazine*, September/October 2009.

Smith, Eric. "Offshore Oil Drilling Might Make Environmental Sense," *Washington Post*, April 1, 2010.

Walsh, Bryan. "Vanishing Act: How Climate Change Is Causing a New Age of Extinction," *Time*, Special Environment Issue, April 13, 2009.

Internet Sources

Bailey, Ronald. "Invasion of the Invasive Species: Local Biodiversity Is Increasing," *Reason*, August 10, 2010. http://reason.com/archives/2010/08/10/invasion-of-the-invasive-speci.

Casey, Michael. "Internet Is Biggest Threat to Endangered Species," *Guardian* (Manchester, UK), March 21, 2010. www.guardian.co.uk/environment/2010/mar/21/endangered-species-internet-threat.

Choi, Charles. "Little Fish Exploding in Number: Prey Species Are Growing as Predators Are Wiped Out," National Geographic News, February 25, 2011. http://news.nationalgeographic.com/news/2011/02/110225-little-fish-oceans-environment-fishing.

Convention on Biological Diversity. "Biodiversity in 2010: Species Populations and Extinction Risks," Global Biodiversity Outlook 3, May 10, 2010. http://gbo3.cbd.int/the-outlook/gbo3/biodiversity-in-2010/species-populations-and-extinction-risks.aspx.

Defenders of Wildlife. "Wildlife and Offshore Drilling," August 9, 2010. www.defenders.org/resources/publications/programs_and_policy/wildlife_conservation/threats/wildlife_and_offshore_drilling_coastal_wetlands.pdf.

Derbyshire, David. "Back from the Dead: One Third of 'Extinct' Animals Turn Up Again," *Daily Mail* (London), September 29, 2010. www.dailymail.co.uk/sciencetech/article-1315964/One-extinct-animals-turn-again.html.

Hemingway, Mark. "Big Green Regulations Suffocate Jobs, Economic Growth," *Washington Examiner*, September 27, 2010. www.washingtonexaminer.com/opinion/columns/special-editorial-reports/Special-report-Big-Green-regulations-suffocate-jobs-economic-growth-103846204.html.

Lane, Carol. "Rescuing Optimism," Conservation International, June 5, 2008. www.conservation.org/FMG/Articles/Pages/rescuing_plan_to_save_pandas.aspx.

Lewis, Mario, Jr. "Birds, Beetles, Extinctions," *Al Gore's Science Fiction: A Skeptic's Guide to "An Inconvenient Truth,"* CEI Congressional Working Paper, Competitive Enterprise Institute, March 16, 2007. http://cei.org/pdf/5820.pdf.

McClain, Craig. "The Mass Extinction of Scientists Who Study Species," *Wired*, January 19, 2011. www.wired.com/wiredscience/2011/01/extinction-of-taxonomists/#.

McLaughlin, Kathleen E. "Borderland: China's Dangerous Appetite for Rare Animals," *Global Post*, October 26, 2010. www.globalpost.com/dispatch/china/101014/border-trafficking-endangered-species-animals.

Messenger, Stephen. "GPS Devices Installed in African Rhinos' Horns," *Treehugger*, October 24, 2010. www.treehugger.com/files/2010/10/gps-devices-installed-in-african-rhinos-horns.php?campaign=daily_nl#.

Miller, Max. "Dangerous Ideas: Let Elephants and Lions Roam the Great Plains," Big Think, August 30, 2010. http://bigthink.com/ideas/22985.

National Wildlife Federation. "How Animals Fight Global Warming," January 6, 2010. www.nwf.org/News-and-Magazines/National-Wildlife/Animals/Archives/2010/How-Animals-Fight-Global-Warming.aspx.

O'Carroll, Eoin. "Environment Versus Economy: A False Choice?," *Christian Science Monitor*, November 5, 2008. www.csmonitor.com/Environment/Bright-Green/2008/1105/environment-versus-economy-a-false-choice.

Raloff, Janet. "When to Welcome 'Invading' Species: Climate Refugees Challenge Environmental Distinctions Between Friend and Foe," *ScienceNews*, October 25, 2010. www.sciencenews.org/view/generic/id/64704/title/When_to_welcome_%E2%80%98invading%E2%80%99_species.

Rogers, Kara. "Biodiversity Decline and the Spread of Infectious Disease," Talking Science, December 14, 2010. www.talkingscience.org/2010/12/biodiversity-decline-and-the-spread-of-infectious-disease.

Rufus, Anneli. "Endangered Species on the Grill: The Black Market in Illegal Meat Flourishes in the U.S.," *AlterNet*, February 15, 2010. www.alternet.org/food/145668/waiter,_there's_an_endangered_rat_snake_in_my_soup!_snooping_into_the_bloody_black_market_for_wild_meat.

Schiermeier, Quirin. "Biodiversity's Ills Not All Down to Climate Change," *Nature*, March 20, 2011. www.nature.com/news/2011/110320/full/news.2011.170.html.

Schmidt, Brian. "Understanding the Endangered Species Act: The Unauthorized Biography of a Tiger Salamander," Committee for Green Foothills, Updated September 13, 2010. www.greenfoothills.org/news/2004/07-2004_SalamanderBio.html.

Shows, Ronnie. "Can Business and Environmentalism Coexist?," *Daily Caller*, March 26, 2010. http://dailycaller.com/2010/03/26/can-business-and-environmentalism-coexist/print/.

Stahl, Lesley. "Could Extinct Species Make a Comeback?," *60 Minutes*, CBS News, January 10, 2010. www.cbsnews.com/stories/2010/01/07/60minutes/main6067594.shtml.

US Fish & Wildlife Service. "Federally Listed Wildlife and Plants Threatened by Gulf Oil Spill," June 2010. www.fws.gov/home/dhoilspill/pdfs/FedListedBirdsGulf.pdf.

Virgo, Paul. "Biodiversity: Not Just About Tigers and Pandas," *Truthout*, May 23, 2010. www.truth-out.org/biodiversity-not-just-about-tigers-and-pandas59760.

Ward, Chip. "The Big Bad Wolf Makes Good," *Mother Jones*, September 28, 2010. http://motherjones.com/environment/2010/09/yellowstone-wolf-reintroduction.

Zimmer, Carl. "First Comes Global Warming, Then an Evolutionary Explosion," *Yale Environment 360*, August 3, 2009. http://e360.yale.edu/content/feature.msp?id=2178.

Index

A
Agence France-Presse (AFP), 50
Agriculture, industrialized, 66
Amphibians, 16
ANWR (Arctic National Wildlife Reserve), 80
Arctic, loss of sea ice in, 60
Arctic National Wildlife Reserve (ANWR), 80
Australia, 15–16, 17

B
Bachman's warbler, 26
Bailey, Ronald, 40, 78
Bald eagles, *89*, 89–90
Bamboo/bamboo forest ecosystems, *99*
  role of giant panda in, *99*, 103, 105
Barataria Bay (LA), 71–72, *72*
  impact of *Deepwater Horizon* oil spill on, 73–74
Barnosky, Anthony, 8
Basic Oil Spill Cost Estimation Model (Environmental Protection Agency), 82
Bears. *See* Grizzly bears; Polar bears
Benzene, 73
Biodiversity
  loss of, has disastrous consequences for humankind, 28–35
  role in mitigation of climate change, 58–59
  threat of loss is exaggerated, 28–35
Blomberg, Simon, 24
BP oil spill (2010). *See Deepwater Horizon* oil spill
Brachiopods, 15
Budiansky, Stephen, 20

C
Campbell, Hank, 9
Carbon dioxide (CO_2)
  atmospheric levels of, 17
  deforestation/land use change and, 58
  plant growth response to increase in atmospheric levels of, 65
  sequestering of, 58
Carolina parakeet, 26
Charismatic megafauna, 98, 103
Chisholm, Sally, 32
Cities
  effects of species loss on, 56–58

Index 125

measures to respond to/
  mitigate climate change
  in, 61
Climate change
  extinction events caused by,
    7–8
  is a significant threat to
    plant/animal species,
    55–62, 99–100
  plant/animal species can
    adapt to, 63–69
  See also Global warming
Clinton, Bill, *89*
CO_2. *See* Carbon dioxide
Conniff, Richard, 28
Convention on Biodiversity
  (Japan, 2010), *52*
Convention on Biological
  Diversity, 44
Corwin, Jeff, 8–9
Countdown 2010, 55

D
Dall, William T., 35
DDT, 90, 92
Deepwater Horizon (BP) oil
  spill (2010), 70, 71, 79
  clean up costs for, 82–83
  effects on dolphins, 72–73
  species threatened by, 76
Deforestation
  in Brazil, *25, 26, 59*
  in China, 105
  rate of, has declined, 38–39
Dinosaurs, 8

Dolphins, 71
  effects of oil spills on,
    72–73
  of Yangtze River, extinction
    of, 100
Drugs, impact of species loss
  on discovery of, 33–35,
  105
DuHamel, Jonathan, 95

E
Eagles. *See* Bald eagles
Ecological Economics (journal),
  32
Economics of Ecosystems and
  Biodiversity (TEEB) report
  (United Nations), 41
Ecosystem services, 32
Ehrlich, Paul, 23
Endangered Species Act
  (ESA, 1973)
  is effective, 86–92
  is not effective, 93–96
  number of species removed
    from, 95
End-Cretaceous extinction, 8,
  13, *14*
End-Devonian extinction, 7,
  14
End-Permian extinction, 7,
  14, 15, 18
Energy Economics (journal),
  80
Environmental Protection
  Agency (EPA), 82

ESA. *See* Endangered Species
　　Act
Extinction(s)
　　is natural part of life,
　　　　99–100
　　IUCN Red List is a flawed
　　　　measure of risk of, 43–49
　　IUCN Red List is world's
　　　　best measure of risk of,
　　　　43–49
　　recent, *30–31*
　　See also Mass extinction(s)
Exxon Valdez oil spill (1989),
　　72, 73, 83
　　clean up costs for, 83

F
Falcons. *See* Peregrine falcons
Fangliang He, 53
FAO (UN Food and
　　Agriculture Organization),
　　38
Fish and Wildlife Service,
　　US, 87, 88
Fisher, Diana, 24
Florida panthers, *39*, 40,
　　90

G
Genyornis newtoni (flightless
　　bird), 15, 17
Ghazoul, Jaboury, 38
Giant pandas, *106*
　　cost for zoos to host, 98,
　　　　100

　　as charismatic megafauna,
　　　　98, 103, 104
　　historical/current habitat
　　　　of, *104*
　　should be left to go extinct,
　　　　97–101
　　should not be left to go
　　　　extinct, 102–107
　　US zoos displaying, *100*
"Global Forest Resources
　　Assessment 2010" (UN
　　Food and Agriculture
　　Organization), 38–39
Global warming, 18, 41
　　species will benefit from,
　　　　66–67
　　See also Climate change
Gore, Al, 22
Gray wolves, 90–91
Grizzly bears, 91
Gulf of Mexico
　　animal life in, by depth, *75*
　　environmental problems in,
　　　　74, 76
　　See also Deepwater Horizon
　　　　oil spill

H
Habitat loss
　　calculation of effects on
　　　　species, 52–53
　　due to deforestation,
　　　　predictions of, 22–24
　　species are most threatened
　　　　by, 64

Hahn, Robert, 80, 82
Hawaii, 16–17
Heywood, Vernon, 24–25
Hilton-Taylor, Craig, 43
Hoffman, Doug L., 36
Holocene extinction event, 9
Hubbell, Stephen, 51, 52, 53
Humans, role in mass
  extinction events, 15–17

I
Intergovernmental Panel on
  Climate Change (IPCC),
  51
International Union for
  Conservation of Nature
  (IUCN)
  World Congress of, 45
International Union for the
  Conservation of Nature
  (IUCN), 16
International Year of
  Biodiversity (United
  Nations), 37
IPCC (Intergovernmental
  Panel on Climate Change),
  51
IUCN (International Union
  for the Conservation of
  Nature), 16
The IUCN Red List of
  Threatened Species
  (International Union
  for the Conservation of
  Nature)
  is a flawed measure of
    extinction risk, 50–53
  is world's best measure of
    extinction risk, 43–49
Ivory-billed woodpeckers,
  26

K
Kemp's Ridley sea turtles,
  76
Knoll, Andrew, 18–19
Kolbert, Elizabeth, 12

L
Late Ordovician extinction,
  7, 13, *14*
Leakey, Richard, 15
Leopold, Aldo, 33
Lorenz, Konrad, 105

M
MacPhee, Ross, 16
Madagascar, 16
Manatees, 76
Mass extinction(s)
  in earth's history, 7–8, 13,
    14, 15
  is imminent, 12–19
  predictions of, are
    unfounded, 20–27
May, Robert M., 37–38
Mencken, Henry Louis, 42
Moas, 16, 17
Moore, Patrick, 9
Myers, Norman, 22

N

National Center for Policy Analysis, 93
National Geographic (magazine), 98
National Marine Fisheries Service, US, 87, 88
National Oceanic and Atmospheric Administration (NOAA), 76
National Snow and Ice Data Center, 60
National Wildlife Federation (NWF), 86
Natural Resources Defense Council (NRDC), 80
Nature (journal), 8, 51
New Zealand, 16, 40
Newman, David J., 33–34
Newman, Mark, 7, 8
NOAA (National Oceanic and Atmospheric Administration), 76
Normal Accidents (Perrow), 84

O

Obama administration, 80
Oceans, drop in pH level of, 17, 18
Offshore oil drilling
  benefits outweigh risks to wildlife, 78–84
  endangers wildlife, 70–77
  public support for, 80
Offshore oil platforms, *81*
Opinion polls. *See* Surveys

P

Packer, Craig, 40
Packham, Chris, 97, 103
Pandas. *See* Giant pandas
Panthers. *See* Florida panthers
Passell, Peter, 80, 82
Peregrine falcons, 92
Perrow, Charles, 84
Petroleum discharges, by sources, *83*
Polar bears, 67–68
  effects of loss of sea ice on, 60
Polls. *See* Surveys
PR Newswire (news service), 93
Prochlorococcus (bacteria), *32*

R

Rabalais, Nancy, 74, 76
Rain forests, Amazon Basin
  clearing of, *59*
  extent of deforestation, *25*
The Rational Optimist (Ridley), 21
Reason (magazine), 78
Red List. *See* The IUCN Red List of Threatened Species
Red-cockaded woodpeckers, 92
Reichholf, Josef, 63

The Resilient Earth
(Mencken), 42
Ridley, Matt, 21

S
Sakashita, Miyoko, 79
Science (journal), 37, 38
Sea turtles. *See* Kemp's Ridley sea turtles
Seasholes, Brian, 93, 94, 95
Solé, Richard V., 7, 8
Species
  are most threatened by habitat loss, 64
  criteria for listing on Endangered Species List, 88
  effects of climate change on, 56
  global warming will benefit, 66–67
  importance of, 29, 32
  number removed from Endangered Species Act, 95
  numbers listed as threatened/endangered in US, 87
  numbers recovered after being listed as extinct, 24
  percent assessed for IUCN Red List, 45
  recent extinctions of, *30–31*
Species Information Services (SIS), 46
Species-area relationship, 22, 23–26, 52–53
Sperm whales, 76
Spiegel (magazine), 63
Steadman, David, 17
Steiner, Rick, 72–73, 74
Stern, Nicholas, 82
Stuart, Simon N., 43
Surveys
  on major environmental concerns, *41*
  on support for offshore oil drilling, 80
Sutherland, Bill, 105

T
Taxol, 33, 34
TEEB report (Economics of Ecosystems and Biodiversity report, United Nations), 41
Threatened species, numbers of, by continent, *47*

U
United Nations, 37
United Nations Food and Agriculture Organization (FAO), 38
Usborne, Simon, 102

V
Valentine, Iain, 105
Vie, J.C., 43
Vultures, 32

W
Warbler. *See* Bachman's warbler
Weather, climate change and, 59–60
Whitty, Julia, 70
Wilson, E.O., 22–23
Wolong Natural Nature Reserve (China), 105
Wolves, 39–40. *See also* Gray wolves
Woodpeckers. *See* Ivory-billed woodpeckers; Red-cockaded woodpeckers
World Congress of the International Union for Conservation of Nature (IUCN), *45*
Wrens, *68*

Y
Yew tree, 33–34, *34*

Picture Credits

AP Images/Dita Alangkara, 85
AP Images/Gerald Herbert, 72
AP Images/Wally Santana, 34
AP Images/Gregory Smith, 39
AP Images/Susan Walsh, 89
© blickwinkel/Alamy, 68
Field Museum Library/Getty Images, 18
Gale/Cengage Learning, 14, 30–31, 41, 47, 65, 75, 83, 100, 104
Albert Gea/Reuters/Landov, 11, 45
Kyodo/Landov, 52, 106
M-Sat Ltd/Photo Researchers, Inc., 25
© Edward Parker/Alamy, 59
© Neil Lee Sharp/Alamy, 81
USCG/Landov, 54
Gao Xueyu/Xinhua/landov, 99